Philanthropy Reconsidered

PRIVATE INITIATIVES – PUBLIC GOOD – QUALITY OF LIFE

George McCully

A Catalogue for Philanthropy Publication

AuthorHouse™
1663 Liberty Drive, Suite 200
Bloomington, IN 47403
www.authorhouse.com
Phone: 1-800-839-8640

First published by AuthorHouse   8/22/2008

ISBN: 978-1-4389-0561-7 (sc)
ISBN: 978-1-4389-0562-4 (hc)
ISBN: 978-1-4389-0563-1 (e)

Printed in the United States of America
Bloomington, Indiana

This book is printed on acid-free paper.

Contents

Acknowledgements

This book would not exist without the *Catalogue for Philanthropy,* and all the talented and resourceful people and institutions that have contributed to its success. The *Catalogue*'s primary mission is education; quantifiers evaluating the *Catalogue*'s effectiveness should therefore reckon that this one book summarizes what at least one philanthropist has learned writing eleven *Catalogues*.

The *Catalogue,* in turn, would not exist without the support and encouragement of the Trustees of the Ellis L. Phillips Foundation, with whom I have served for twenty years, also learning a great deal. I am especially indebted to Larry Phillips, Walter Paine, and Cornelia Grumman, who strongly supported the *Catalogue* from its birth.

For practical assistance and moral support in all aspects of publication, I thank the Trustees of the *Catalogue* and its senior staff: Carl Mastandrea (COO and Managing Editor) and Wendy Connors (Director of Development); Maureen Crocker of Crocker Design, a true believer; my friend Andy Stewart for legal and publishing advice; and from their diverse areas of expertise, my sons Nat, Tad, and Philip, and daughter Katie McCully.

Thanks also to readers of the manuscript at various stages: Rusty Aertsen, Hale Andrews, Bill Davlin, Angie Eikenberry, David Ford, Laura Gang, Pat Gray, Scottie Held, Susanah Howland, Amy Kass, Ruth Martin, Michele Mittelman, Clarissa Porter, and Julia Toulmin. For scholarly suggestions in the field of Classics I am especially grateful to my recently discovered colleague at Indiana University, Marty Sulek; because I have not always followed his advice, as well as on general principles, any errors of scholarship in that field and others are mine alone, and I welcome their correction by readers. For personal support I am forever grateful to Barbara Ardan.

Introduction

This small book ranges rather widely, over large and diverse subjects, to illuminate what is happening in American philanthropy today, and what it all means. Though its scope is quite spacious, extending into scholarly and even philosophic realms, its purpose is practical—focusing ultimately on the central questions of philanthropy: How can, and why should, we do good?

Chapter I, "Promethean Fire: the Archetype," defines the concept of "philanthropy" by reference to its original etymology and history in Classical Greek, Roman, Judeo-Christian and early-medieval times. The Classical concept of "*philanthropia*" originated as a humanistic (in the Classical sense) model and ideal, associated with civic culture and education, or self-development.

Needless to say, that philosophical dimension and depth have been lost. For a modern definition faithful to these roots we propose "**private initiatives for public good, focusing on quality of life.**" This is close to definitions already widely respected—e.g., John Gardner's "private initiative for the public good," Bob Payton's "voluntary action for the public good," Lester Salamon's "the private giving of time or valuables…for public purposes," *et al.* By yoking modern definitions to original etymology and history, we hope to ground them more firmly and authoritatively in the long and authentic cultural tradition.

We use (public) "good" as referring objectively to the benefactors' **intentions**. This is crucial (for example, it excludes acts of terrorism). Here it has no normative or unscientific meaning, because it does not evaluate anything.

Our last phrase, "focusing on quality of life," agrees with Robert Bremner's assertion that "the aim of philanthropy...is improvement in the quality of human life." We, however, emphasize that philanthropy purportedly enhances quality of life for **both** benefactors and beneficiaries, which has long been recognized as philanthropy's primary appeal. Whereas relatively few people today care about "philanthropy" as such (in large part because they do not know what the word means), all surveys indicate that what people do care about and want most is "quality of life." This is what philanthropy in the Classical tradition is all about. Philanthropy is a tried and true—it has been argued, the best—way to achieve it. This first chapter seeks a consensus view because definitions matter, as the next chapter proves.

Chapter II, "Philanthropy's Finest Hour: the American Revolution," is about American philanthropy—generally considered the strongest in the world. We show that the "philanthropy" which achieved its highest expression here was—explicitly and significantly—the Classical model, applied through voluntary associations, which were routine in Colonial America. The Classical view supplied the conceptual model, and voluntary associations the institutional and procedural model, for the American Revolution and Constitution. It was in this context that philanthropy became a fundamental cause, inspiration, and formative influence on the American Revolution, which we say consisted in the application of philanthropic routines to national politics, and particularly nation-building.

Philanthropy created the United States of America as purportedly a philanthropic nation, and is therefore quintessentially American. The Founding Fathers considered it a leading argument for the Constitution. It may be the best explanation for the widely accepted superiority of our Founders. It explains why they believed this could be both a good and great nation—a truly philanthropic nation, ideally benefiting all mankind in both principle and practice.

Robert Bremner and many others have noticed connections between the 18th-century Enlightenment, philanthropic ideals, and the American Revolution. Where this analysis breaks new ground is in pointing out how the Colonists' previous 150 years of practical and philosophical experience with the philanthropy of voluntary associations, virtually taught them how and why to create, by their distinctively American Revolution, a new philanthropic nation. This interpretation illuminates many details about our Revolution, as well as why it failed to be replicated in Europe, where leaders and citizens lacked our practical experience in philanthropy, and had less salutary models to follow. In this sense the ancient tag, "philanthropic and democratic," used to describe both Socrates and the Laws of Athens, was once again confirmed as a bonded pair.

Chapter III, "Philanthropy Yesterday and Today," concerns more familiar territory: modern practical philanthropy—how in the last half of the twentieth century, philanthropy in America achieved, technically and institutionally, a distinctive, modern, paradigmatic form. In the context of Chapters I and II however, we note that the 20th-century paradigm lacked the Classical, and classical American, deeper understanding of philanthropy—focusing on technical and procedural issues while neglecting intellectual or philosophical content.

As the 20th century closed, that paradigm entered a period of fundamental transformation—a paradigm-shift—which is still going on. The causes and onset of the transformation identify it clearly as a paradigm-shift—a characteristic type of historical change that contains seeds of the next paradigm, which is to say the future of philanthropy.

Thus Chapters I and II illuminate the deeper significance of what is happening today. With American philanthropy now thoroughly in flux, we can and should "reconsider" philanthropy, to reflect more deeply on what it is and can be, ideally—essentially, historically, personally, and culturally.

Chapter IV, "The Future of Philanthropy," continues the paradigm-shift analysis to suggest some issues facing a few exemplary Old Paradigm institutions—e.g., large charities, large traditional foundations, national professional associations, and federated giving programs. Discernible innovative trends within the paradigm-shift, that are driven by advancing technology, are also discussed: philanthropy becoming more visible and accessible, and therefore prominent and influential; data rapidly multiplying; increasing knowledge management; and systematization.

Chapter V, "Philanthropy Reborn," envisions some of the practical implications of this entire book's argument for various constituencies in and around philanthropy—donors, grantmakers, trustees, philanthropic advisors, financial advisors, fundraisers, executive directors, scholars, teachers, students, journalists, religious, civic and political leaders. If Classical American philanthropy is reborn, so that philanthropy itself is enlarged as a cultural phenomenon; and if the infrastructure and modes of operation of philanthropy are empowered by the new technology driving the current paradigm-shift; philanthropy can become a popular movement and cultural influence—our school for values, in this renewed philanthropic nation.

Appendix One: "Case Study: the *Catalogue for Philanthropy* System in Massachusetts" presents as an example of the paradigm-shift in action, the emerging *Catalogue* system, which has been designed specifically to solve problems at the interface between the Old Paradigm and the public (who provide 85% of the private dollars in philanthropy), and to strengthen the culture of philanthropy—its vocabulary, conceptualization, rhetoric, infrastructure, and modes of operation. Through donor education and the creation of innovative donor-friendly tools, we intend to promote Classical American philanthropy in perpetuity, to increase and improve charitable giving significantly.

Appendix Two: "A Taxonomy for Philanthropy," contains what is to our knowledge the first graphic illustration of philanthropy as a whole, taken from the 2007 *Catalogue*. There are innumerable lists of fields in philanthropy, usually associated with directories of grantmakers and their funding interests. Because the categories organizing those lists are not systematic—i.e., logically related—they are technically not taxonomies. This limits their value in donor education, data collection and analysis, and comparisons between philanthropic markets, and leads to instability of field lists over time. The *Catalogue*'s proposed taxonomy is very much a work-in-progress, being developed collaboratively with the charities of Massachusetts on our website, *www.cfp-ma.org*. The challenge is enormously complex intellectually and technically, not least because a taxonomy of philanthropy is also a taxonomy of quality-of-life. We welcome all constructive assistance.

Appendix Three: "Bibliographic Notes" is not exhaustive or definitive, but more an indication of significant references that helped me develop the views expressed in this book. I regret that I could not name, much less remember, all of my teachers on these many and varied subjects.

What we are offering here, in short, is a strategic overview of philanthropy—and the same time a basic "primer" on what it is, that can also serve as a basic introduction for understanding what it is, what it has accomplished, where it is today, where it is going, and in each case, how and why. The variety of subjects treated here, and our focus on their interconnections, are needed to describe and understand our subject adequately, as a single whole.

The purpose of all this is to "reconsider philanthropy." At a time when philanthropy is dramatically changing; and when our failures to define terms precisely, to get beyond crude IRS data and terminology, to conduct ourselves wisely, and to teach the public about philanthropy, are hurting us in poorly conceived court decisions, tax assessments, and government regulations; we need to think it all through, once more—to have a serious conversation about philanthropy among scholars, practitioners, legislators, judges, and the public. The purpose of this book is to help promote that conversation.

We cordially invite assenting and dissenting views constructively expressed on the *Catalogue's* blog at our website, *www.cfp-ma.org.*

φ

I. Promethean Fire: the Archetype

A. Context

Very few people today, even professionals, know what the word "philanthropy" means, or how it relates to charitable giving. I have posed the question at professional meetings, and found that not only are there almost as many definitions as there are people in the room, but that few if any care what it means—they see no particular value in defining it. Until recently, it was rarely used; many considered it too fancy and even pretentious for ordinary purposes, so they inclined to the much simpler word and concept, "giving." Today, though it has become a household word—which is good—its meaning is still lost; folks use it to refer loosely to charitable giving or organizations (which is a start), or worse, to the "non-profit," "voluntary," or "social" "sector."

This is how great ideas die, which is in this case tragic, because in truth "philanthropy" has a clear, powerful, inspiring, donor-friendly, meaning and history, which we would do well now to revive.

There are three main ways to define words: by conventional usage—what most ordinary people mean when they use it; by etymology—analysis of its parts in root languages; and/or by its history, carefully selecting the more useful precedents. Usually these methods are combined, trying to be reasonable, practical, and significantly useful, while avoiding pedantry on the one hand or banality on the other. With "philanthropy" the confusion and chaos of current usage needs correction by etymology and history.

B. Etymology and the Original Story

First let's unpack the etymology, which is fairly well-known. "Philanthropy" combines two Greek words, *philos* and *anthropos. Philos*, generally understood as related to "love," is familiar to us in words like "philosophy" (love of wisdom) and Philadelphia (brotherly love), and any number of "phil-" words. Aristotle, in his *Nicomachean Ethics*, defined the verb form as wanting or doing for someone what one thinks good for that person, as distinct from doing it for one's own selfish reasons—what we might call "generous benefaction." Aristotle also thought that *philia* was necessary for happiness, and was in itself noble. We take these Aristotelian references to be indicative rather than definitive for all earlier and later usages, because he was defining the term for philosophical rather than vernacular purposes. *Anthropos* with which we are familiar from "anthropology" (the study of mankind), referred to humanity or all mankind (it did not distinguish between men and women). Combining these roots, then, we have something like "love of humanity" or "love of mankind," involving "generous benefaction" and "happiness."

As for the word's history, when, by whom, and why, were these root words originally combined? Who was the first "philanthropist"? Though "first use" always implies "so far as we know," and there is some recent scholarly controversy about the particular authorship—which needn't detain us because we are relying only on the text itself—the word was probably coined, and again probably by Aeschylus, the first great playwright of ancient Greece, in his *Prometheus Bound* (ca. 460 BCE). Prometheus, according to myth, was the Titan who created mankind out of clay. His creatures, however, were at first not inspiring; they had no knowledge, nor skills of any kind, and consequently lived in caves, in darkness, in constant fear for their lives. Zeus, the tyrannical king of the gods, was not impressed, and decided to destroy them. But Prometheus, out of his "*philanthropos tropos*"— his "humanity-loving character" [lines 11, 28]—gave to his creatures two gifts (lines 250-258): fire, symbolizing all knowledge, arts, sciences, technology and practical skills—everything that makes possible and constitutes civilization; and "blind (i.e. unknowing) hope," or optimism. These two gifts go together, as a complementary and mutually-reinforcing pair. With fire, optimism is justified; optimism motivates using "fire" to improve the human condition.

Many people have thought that this "love of mankind" definition empties the word of all practical meaning and renders it useless—for if it means loving everybody, and no ordinary mortal loves everybody, none of us can be philanthropists. That understanding, however, would make the coinage absurd, so we should try harder to understand it.

The word as originally coined could not possibly have referred to loving all humans as individuals, because Prometheus' *philanthropos tropos* **preceded** the existence of individuality. At that mythical point in time the creatures that would become humans were living like animals, in caves, without any individuating knowledge or skills. The whole point was that they lacked full "humanity," and it was their distinctively human potential that Prometheus loved—what those cave-dwellers could make of themselves with fire and optimism, or what we might call "humane-ness." In fact, Cicero and others later translated the Greek word *philanthropia* into Latin as *humanitas* (see below). Full humanity, as a value-laden term, thus begins with philanthropy—loving it in the sense of caring about, seeking, and nourishing, human potential, or what it is to be human.

Or to consider another current absurdity, at a fairly recent national professional meeting the head of a major foundation was reported to believe (regrettably he was not there to defend himself) that the word "philanthropy" was originally sexist—referring only to men and excluding women. Again, the original coinage shows why the word was not sexist—because that interpretation would deprive the word of its purpose and meaning in the play.

Now obviously, the playwright coined the phrase for his own and his immediate audience's purposes, not ours. We are interested in his usage because we might learn from it for our purposes. We are not required or obliged to understand it in any one way, much less because he was trying to teach us anything, but because we, thinking about it as both myth and lesson, might learn and benefit from it.

To do so, we shall consider it here on three levels: first, as **myth**—a meaningful story for Greek culture; second, as **history**—how the word and its idea gained broader meaning, evoking other significant and edifying usages; and third, as its having **practical meaning** for us and our "philanthropy," now and in the future.

C. Myth

It is significant that this first known usage occurs in the context of Greek mythology, religion and literature, rather than in mundane practical instances; this immediately associates it with ideas, on a lofty plane, significantly beyond general or specific acts of "giving."

Aeschylus (or the playwright) was proposing Prometheus' "philanthropy" to explain what made humans different from all other creatures—what made and makes us distinctively human. The difference, he was saying, what plainly distinguishes us from all other animals, is our culture or civilization—our knowledge and skills, which improve our lives and living conditions. Here he was reformulating in more capacious framework an earlier Prometheus myth of Hesiod's, to help explain the emergence of humanity—how distinctively **human** history began.

He said, and to this we should closely attend, that human history and civilization began with, and depend upon, *philanthropia*—a love of what it is to be human, of all those attributes that can make life distinctively humane. Prometheus' philanthropy, in effect, completed his creation of humankind —empowering and enhancing humanity as good, respectable, and capable of progress.

There are particular points to be noted in all this:

- The name "Prometheus," meant "forethought" or "foresight"—the ability to think ahead, or see into the future; in the myth only Prometheus and his mother, Earth, had it, but it is an essential attribute—characteristic of—philanthropists, who must be forward-looking.

- The word "philanthropic" was originally an adjective, not a noun or verb; it modified not the gift, nor even the giving, but the personal attitude, character, or disposition of the donor.

- The notable phenomenon for which Aeschylus may even have invented this expression, was a motivating feeling leading to doing good—benefaction—an act of **general, principled,** benevolence on the part of the donor, not merely for his own advantage, or that of his family, neighbors, tribe or even nation, but for the enhancement of humanity itself—*anthropos*—the essence of being human, a new kind of essence or being, the human condition, which Prometheus had created.

- The "love" referred to—*philia*—was not merely felt, thought, or stated, but **rendered**—acted upon, in benefaction—**doing** good.

- The benefaction was freely voluntary—not obliged as a duty (moral or otherwise), nor extracted from the donor/benefactor by any outside influence (e.g., aggressive fundraising). It was initiated, originated, by the donor himself, expressing his character and thus defining himself by value-intensive, voluntary action.

- The gifts were not just vaguely "good" for the beneficiaries, but—more precisely—empowering: increasing their competencies and improving their lives and prospects on every level, as human beings.

- This philanthropic empowerment was not just personal; it changed the course of history. The gifts of fire and optimism were civilizing and en-nobling, enabling humans, as Aeschylus himself put it, to emerge from caves, from darkness into light, to fulfill their uniquely human potential. "All the arts that mortals have come from Prometheus." (506)

- The gifts were also mutually reinforcing—"fire" and "blind hope" or optimism together produced progress, proceeding hand-in-hand, each nourishing the other.

- Zeus, the tyrannical king of the gods, had no *philanthropos tropos*, and had apparently planned to destroy Prometheus' creatures. Prometheus stole the fire from Mt. Olympus, rebelling against Zeus' rule (which he had helped establish), so Zeus punished him—showing that Prometheus did not do it for his own advantage. In this case, Zeus had Prometheus chained to a rock in the Caucasus, and sent an eagle to devour his liver daily; Titans being immortal, it grew back at night. This gruesome ordeal lasted 30,000 years, but for our purposes as well as for the Greeks, this key component of the story yoked philanthropy with freedom and democracy, against tyranny. Pre-Enlightenment Christian iconography portrayed Prometheus as a Christ-figure, nobly and redemptively suffering out of his love for all mankind; with the Enlightenment Prometheus became a symbol for freedom and progress.

Beyond these details, the story had many implications on which there is less agreement because the authoritative texts have been lost. *Prometheus Bound* was the first (or perhaps second) of three connected plays, a trilogy known as the *Prometheia*, of which one is lost and we have only fragments of the third. Scholars have tried to fill the gaps from references to them by other ancient writers, and inferences from the surviving fragments, supplemented by general knowledge of Aeschylean tragedy and other Greek drama.

Among the inferences, there are reasons to believe that Zeus himself eventually forgave Prometheus, and sent Hercules (Herakles) his (illegitimate) son, to kill the eagle and free Prometheus. The moral superiority of Prometheus' philanthropy, and of his steadfastness in it under excruciating torture, compelled Zeus' respect. Prometheus was also apparently reconciled to Zeus and his more generous reign. Thus philanthropy was associated with heroism, virtue, and the Greek educational ideal of excellence (*aretē*) in all aspects of an individual's life.

This understanding is reinforced by the coherence of the resulting whole story: that Prometheus had created humanity, but that in their primitive state Zeus was not impressed by humans and had decided to destroy them. Prometheus' rebellious gifts of fire and optimism produced technical progress, which proved humanity's worth and rescued them from destruction. When Zeus saw how noble humans could be, and how heroic Prometheus was in his philanthropy, he relented and reconciled himself and his reign to Prometheus' nobler vision.

This interpretation would posit the Promethean model of philanthropy— loving humanity—as crucial not just to human civilization, progress, and freedom, but to human survival on Earth. Loving what it is to be human thus has made us what we are as human beings, and is the key to our quality of life and all we can be.

D. Subsequent History

1. Liberal Education and Humane Culture
The connection of *philanthropia* with education was obvious and immediate—in fact they were thought to be one and the same. Plato, in his early dialogue *Euthyphro* (ca. 390s BCE) presents Socrates saying of himself that owing to his *philanthropia* "I...pour out whatever I possess to every man, not only without pay, but even with pleasure if anyone is willing to listen to me."(3d-e) Plato also, in the *Phaedo* (89 d-e), yoked their opposites, *misanthropia* and *misologia* (hatred of humanity and hatred of reasoning) as having the same cause. The Platonic Academy compiled a philosophical dictionary which was partially reproduced in the authoritative 2nd century AD edition of Plato's works; it listed "*Philanthropia*" as: "A state of well-educated habits

stemming from love of humanity. A state of being productive of benefit to humans. A state of grace. Mindfulness together with good works." (I owe these citations to Marty Sulek—see Appendix Three).

More broadly speaking, in principle the love of humanity has to include, and begins with, the love of one's own humanity—that is, self-development. The Classical Greek educational ideal was life-long self-development—the pursuit of *areté* (excellence) in everything one thought and did. *Areté* consisted in the fullest development, the perfection, of all one's powers, talents, and resources—all those gifts of body, mind and spirit which together distinguish us as human, whose development makes us more fully humane.

This meant the love of wisdom—*philosophia*—both intellectual and practical, in both thought and ethics. "Wisdom" consisted in correct knowledge and just evaluation of all things. Stoic "philosophers"—teachers and lovers of wisdom in thought and practice—especially elaborated the concept as an educational ideal, and Stoicism eventually became the most broadly held philosophical school in the ancient world. Stoics taught that the world (*cosmos*) is a coherent and harmonious whole (universe), rendered so, i.e., ordered, by a single Universal Law and governing power, the *Logos* (the fundamental assumption of science with respect to the material world). They believed, accordingly, that all humans are members of a single family, constituting humanity, and that feelings of compassion and consideration for all humanity, as well as affirmation of what it is to be human, are essential to being human.

Their fundamental ethical doctrine was "Follow Nature"—that is, align yourself with the all-embracing, harmonizing, ordering power of the Universe, according to the *Logos: kata logos*. This meant "loving" humanity not just by cultivating all aspects of one's own humanity to the fullest, but extending that humaneness to all dimensions of one's own life—personal, social, and civic—and doing so in harmony with the ordering power governing the entire Universe, not only ethics (how humans relate to each other), but also culture (all that humans make) as well as nature (the physical environment, given to humans to work with).

In so comprehensive and unifying a frame, this philosophy of education applied not merely to individuals but to societies and polities as well. They, too, should follow the *Logos*. Not just personal ethics, but the laws of a polity, should be based on, continuous, and coherent with, Natural Law—which is what "cosmopolitan" originally meant. Every aspect of family, social, and civic life—all culture and ethics—should be educational, philanthropic, and philosophical (note the power and universal relevance of love, in the sense of *philia*), teaching and promoting humaneness in harmony with Nature and the *Logos*. That is the sense in which both Socrates and the laws of Athens were said to be "philanthropic"—loving, affirming, enhancing, humanity, or humane-ness.

There was a word for this philosophy and phenomenon of culture: *paideia*, from which our word "encyclopaedia" derives (from *enkyklos paideia*, or "all-embracing," "universal" learning or culture). Its essential element was that all aspects of culture exist, and their purpose is, to "study humanity"—i.e., to teach citizens how to become more fully humane. The *studia humanitatis* or studies of humanity, were also known as the "good arts" (*bonae artes*), the liberal arts (*artes liberales*), or the "humane arts" (*artes humanae*). They were the core of the Western tradition of liberal education, of which the goal was excellence (*areté*).

What we call "humaneness" was for the Greeks and Romans, then, synonymous with loving humanity or *philanthropia*. Cicero, one of the greatest Roman Stoics—Senator, orator, philosopher and educator in the first century BCE—authoritatively translated "*philanthropia*" into Latin as *humanitas*. Aulus Gellius, a second-century grammarian, summed all this up as he sought to rescue the educational intensity of the concept from its later dissolution:

> "Those who have spoken Latin and have used the language correctly do not give the word *humanitas* the meaning which it is commonly thought to have… signifying a kind of friendly spirit and good feeling toward all men without distinction. Rather, they give to *humanitas* about the force of the Greek *paideia*, that is, what we call education and training in the good arts (*bonae artes*). Those who earnestly desire and seek these are most highly humane. For pursuit of that kind of knowledge, and the training given by it, have been granted to man alone among the animals, and for that reason it is termed *humanitas*.

All this derived from, and was an elaboration of, Aeschylus' remarkable assertion that "all the arts that mortals have come from Prometheus" (506), and that they are human civilization. Aeschylus was saying that "all the arts"—meaning all mechanical arts: skills, crafts, technical knowledge and the sciences on which those are based—as well as all "liberal" and what we would call "fine arts"—all these things that constitute civilization—are based on and derive from the enhancing, empowering love of humanity symbolized and epitomized by Prometheus' philanthropy, expressed in his metaphorical gifts of fire and optimism. This is more than a mythical-historical statement; it suggests that the arts not only began, but forever originate, from a philanthropic impulse to enhance humanity and benefit humankind. They were and are transmitted with the continuing gifts of (metaphorically speaking) fire and of optimism. This means that arts are intrinsically philanthropic in character, because their purpose and function was (and is) to improve the human condition—what today we call "quality of life."

2. Civic Humanism

Prometheus' *philanthropia* also had significant political dimensions, which were understood by contemporary Greeks. (If Aeschylus was the author, it is notable that he was born of an aristocratic family and fought at both Salamis and Marathon, the epic battles in which the Greek city-states under Athenian leadership defeated the Asiatic Persians, leading to the great age of Periclean Athens—which is when scholars who dispute Aeschylus' authorship believe *Prometheus Bound* was written.)

This theme, of freedom and republican government overcoming tyranny and slavery, is a *leitmotiv* recurring at high points in Western cultural history: Periclean Athens, Republican Rome, the Florentine Renaissance, the European Enlightenment, and the American Revolution. In all these times leaders rallied citizens by appeals to the rhetorical themes of domestic freedom versus tyranny and slavery associated with alien dictatorships. This rhetoric has repeatedly evoked masterpieces of culture—i.e., education and art—that have transcended their times and spoken eloquently to all humans about humanity itself. They have been canonized in the classical tradition of liberal education and civic humanism—needless to say, the word "humanism," used in connection with Classical scholarship and liberal education, has no relation to modern non- or anti-religious movements. The *Prometheia* and other tragedies of Aeschylus were prototypes of this noble tradition.

The association of philanthropy and democracy in civic humanism makes sense. Only if people are basically competent and constructively disposed—and optimistic enough about themselves to create their own democracy and to pursue their own *philanthropia* (in this Classical, technical, humanities, sense), can they be (optimistically) entrusted with freedom and self-government. In Ancient Greece, the phrase "democratic and philanthropic" was a common expression, and in fact both Xenophon and Demosthenes used both words together to describe Socrates and the laws of Athens, respectively. The significance of this connection will be clear in Chapter II, with the American Revolution.

3. *Philanthropia* and History
Aeschylus' myth contained, and perhaps was intended to express, a "philosophy" of events—what we call history. He was saying that *philanthropia* had introduced, and caused, progress in history itself—e.g., the progressive emergence of humanity from cave-dwelling to civilization, through the development of science, technology, and the arts. This "love of humanity" was capable of improving the human condition itself, so that history could be progressive.

It is important that in Aeschylus' own time there was no concept of "history" in the modern sense, meaning "events"; the word *historia* meant simply "inquiry." Herodotus, Aeschylus' near-contemporary, became "the father of history" the discipline, because his *Histories* (inquiries into the nature of reality, including both Nature and events) described the events and explained the significance of the Greeks' victory in the Persian Wars under the leadership of Athens—in fact his interpretation was based on the dialectic between (Greek, Western) freedom and (Persian, Asian) tyranny.

It is also important that the ancient Greeks had no concept of linear "progress" of periods in history; they believed that history tended to repeat itself in cycles like those in nature—e.g., birth, growth, death, decay, etc.

That said, it is nonetheless true that *Prometheus Bound* proposed a theme that would later be elaborated in historical thought the idea of historical progress from lower to higher states of human being—and identified the key to that progress as *philanthropia*: the love, affirmation, and enhancing development of humanity or humaneness.

4. *Philanthropia*, Theology and Religion
Ultimately, the Classical humane concept of philanthropy had cosmological and theological dimensions as well. By positing Prometheus' caring, optimistic, respect for mankind as eventually converting Zeus' contempt for mankind to *philanthropia*, Aeschylus was figuratively connecting and reconciling civilized, philanthropic, humanity with the universe and universal law, in a coherent and harmonious *cosmos*—which was the subject and focus of the Greek *paideia* explained above.

According to this philosophy, humanity's ethical duty and distinction is to live in accordance with the universal *Logos*, or *kata Logos*. If humans align all of their activities harmoniously with the *Logos*—the ordering power governing the entire *cosmos* as a coherent and harmonious whole universe—they would be cosmopolitan—citizens of the *cosmopolis* or Universal Community, in which every aspect of human enterprise is in accordance with the *cosmos*, fulfilling *philanthropia*.

Greek Stoicism, in its cosmological and theological aspects, informed early Christianity, primarily through the works of St. Paul, who was trained as a Stoic. The *Letter to Titus* which used to be attributed to him, described God (3:4) as "philanthropic," for giving His beloved Son to free mankind from the tyrannical burden of sin; it urged Titus to lead the Christians of Crete to align their lives with that loving example. The same philanthropic understanding of God is found also in the *Gospel of John* (3:16), "For God so loved the world, that He gave His only begotten Son...," and in Luke's *Gospel*, when the birth of Jesus is announced to shepherds by angels as expressing God's "good will toward men" (2:14). John's *Gospel,* which was addressed to the Greeks to help them understand the new Judaic religion, began with the startling assertion that God was the *Logos*, and that Christ was the *Logos* "made flesh and dwelt among us" (1:1-3). Christian philanthropy, then, "follows the *Logos*" (God and Christ) in loving mankind. The use of the word and concept of *philanthropia* was of course especially common in the Greek Byzantine, Eastern Orthodox, theological and liturgical tradition.

The Stoic concept of *philanthropia* reached Judaism through the works of Philo (Judaeus) of Alexandria (20BCE-50CE), a contemporary of Jesus' and a Hellenistic (Greek-speaking) Jew who sought to synthesize Greek philosophy and Judaism. His book, *On the Virtues*, contains an extended explanation of *philanthropia* as a core virtue closely related to piety, in which he tried to show how Moses and the Mosaic Law exemplified Stoic philosophy in general and *philanthropia* in particular. As it turned out, Philo had greater influence on early Christianity—which was much more interested in Classical philosophy—through Paul, the author(s) of the Gospel of John, and patristic writers such as Clement (of Alexandria). Josephus, the Jewish historian, frequently used the word and concept of *philanthropia*, but again Judaic theology and liturgy seem not to have appropriated it.

While the philosophical and religious doctrine of loving all mankind was taught for several centuries after the birth of Jesus, the subsequent decline of Rome was increasingly conducive to a different set of Christian doctrines, which eventually came to dominate medieval culture and the practice of charitable giving. The notion of Christian charity—*caritas* in Latin, *agape* in Greek—promoted the ideal of the Christian love of God as deeply altruistic and selfless, epitomized by Jesus' own self-sacrifice to atone for the sins of all mankind, and by the early Christian martyrs persecuted by the Roman authorities. The notion that humans are basically sinful, "prone to evil and slothful in good," selfish, greedy and prideful, nourished that selfless love as the antidote to sin. This is very nearly the opposite of the Classical concept of *philanthropia*.

As Europe entered the so-called Dark Ages, these *caritas* doctrines became very strongly influential, and eventually superseded the Classical concept of *philanthropia*. As the economy of the Roman Empire disintegrated into chaos, practical philanthropy narrowed to poor relief, first by the rich, and when they too declined, by monastic orders following Jesus' example. As conditions of life became increasingly harsh, and the opportunities for human fulfillment shrank and narrowed, the notion of investing in quality of life for all mankind simply became irrelevant and disappeared. The doctrine of the sinfulness of man made increasing sense. In that world-view the idea of philanthropic progress gave way to a sense of futility—after all, if humans are basically sinful, what hope is there of improving the human condition? Social reforms will be undone by corruption—pettiness, selfishness and greed. Only Divine intervention, forgiving our sins, can improve the human condition. These two opposite points of view eventually became the fundamental alternatives of conservatism and progressivism, but for the next few centuries, the Classical concept of philanthropy was dead—or at least buried.

E. Significance for Us: the Classical Concept of Philanthropy Today

All these associations—of philanthropy or love of humanity, with **freedom** against slavery, and **democracy** against tyranny; with **education** as self-development and empowerment, and **civilization** against primitiveness; and with **optimism** and **progress** in history—and the sense that they are all mutually interdependent and reinforcing, constitute what we shall call the **Classical or humane concept of philanthropy**. (We use the word "humane" to avoid the currently controversial word "humanistic," which however would be preferable if it could be understood only in relation to Classical liberal education and the central role therein of the humanities,

Classically conceived.) Needless to say, this conceptualization is very different from our relatively anemic modern interpretations of philanthropy as "rich helping poor," or "caring," or simply "giving."

How shall we express this in modern terms? There are four relatively authoritative definitions of "philanthropy" that come close to the Classical concept, and that might be combined and restated for purposes of consensus. John Gardner's "private initiative for the public good," and Robert Payton's "voluntary action for the public good" are admirably concise, and capture the important distinction and connection between "private" initiative and "public" good. Lester Salamon's "the private giving of time or valuables... for public purposes" adds some useful details, while the historian Robert Bremner's emphasis that "the aim of philanthropy...is improvement in the quality of human life" adds the crucial "quality of life" dimension essential to the Classical view.

Combining these to connect modern philanthropy with its Classical roots, we suggest "private initiatives for public good, focusing on quality of life."

The three essential elements of this precise definition are: "private initiatives," "public good," and "quality of life." These neatly distinguish philanthropy from both government (public initiatives for public good, focusing on law and order, or in a democracy, on equality and justice), and commerce (private initiatives for private profit, focusing on material prosperity). Let us consider each of the three elements in turn.

1. Private Initiatives
"Private initiatives" means that the benefactors, whether individuals or institutions, voluntarily decide to do something as independent agents, apart from government—as Prometheus had originally done on his own, apart from Zeus. In medieval society there was no distinction between public and private sectors; government was by the kings and nobles, but their realms were considered their private property. In modern society, the idea of the State as a public thing (*res publica*) was revived from Classical thought, creating a division between public and private spheres or sectors. Public initiatives occur when governments and government officials act officially and formally in accordance with laws and Constitutions. They can certainly do good, even in the same fields as philanthropy, but the difference between a private and a public initiative is in this terminology categorical and clear. Paying taxes—even for human services—is not, and is no substitute for, philanthropy, because doing so is required by law, and failure to do so is

officially prosecuted and punished. While it is generally "good" to pay taxes, and government programs thus supported may improve quality of life, the difference from philanthropy is clear and significant.

Scholars sometimes have difficulty deciding whether a charitable corporation is public or private. Does an institution become "public" if government officials participate in its governance? Not so long as it was created and operates by "private initiative." Are "public" charities that receive or are dependent on government grants, philanthropy? Yes, if they were privately initiated and the grants are sought by private initiative (i.e., the government does not require them to apply for or to accept the grants). Can governments create charitable corporations? Yes, and those may be philanthropic if, when, and to the extent that, they are "private" rather than "governmental."

2. Public Good
"Doing good," "benefaction," and similar ideas have always been essential to concepts of philanthropy. Nonetheless, "public good" cannot be defined specifically or by reference to particular criteria, or by any single authority, because obviously people's ideas of public good are matters of taste, differ quite widely, and frequently conflict. We have therefore retained the word "good" as referring objectively to the **intention** of the private initiator(s), grounded in their understanding of love of humaneness, which is crucial; here it has no normative or unscientific significance, and makes no evaluative statement about the results of the initiatives.

Accordingly, in law the "public good" that philanthropy does, for which its activities receive tax exemption and donors receive tax deductions, is defined generally, by broad fields of activity—scientific, educational, religious, etc.

Within those broad limits, **donors' intentions** are also important. Regardless of whether others may agree about means and ends, is the benefactor **intending** to improve quality of life for the beneficiaries? Is it done out of love for humaneness, or some other impulse, with some other agenda? Naturally, problematic cases arise, for example in which a private initiative opposes a widely accepted value or custom. As we shall see in the next chapter, every political and social reform movement in American history has begun as philanthropy, and some were deemed quite unreasonable, undesirable, or even outrageous, by many citizens at first—e.g., women's suffrage, prohibition, or environmentalism, even civil rights. Ideas of public good also change from time to time—often as a result of philanthropic initiatives.

How far can this be pushed—can philanthropic acts violate laws? Yes—Prometheus' original philanthropy was a protest against Zeus himself, the king of the gods. But illegal acts are philanthropic only when they are intended to confer a public, as distinct from a private, benefit.

Yet there are limits. Are terrorist acts philanthropic? No, because although they are private initiatives intended to achieve what the perpetrator believes is a public good, they do not express love of humanity, which is essential in "philanthropy." Terrorism is unqualifiedly misanthropic—the opposite of philanthropy.

Are acts specifically directed to benefit one's immediate or extended family, or circle of friends, philanthropic? This may surprise some people, but: no—because although highly desirable and commendable, those are private initiatives primarily for private benefits, as distinct from public benefits. "Public" benefits begin precisely beyond the boundaries of one's own personal world, where neither oneself nor one's relatives or friends are the intended primary beneficiaries.

Does this mean that philanthropic acts must not benefit the benefactor? Not at all—there are enormous personal benefits in being philanthropic. To begin with, in this Classical humane, or humanistic, tradition the "love of humanity" (i.e. of what it is to be human) is fundamentally educational—self-developing, strengthening and refining one's values and skills through their exercise, which enhances one's own humanity. Beyond that, from Aristotle and beyond, as we shall see in the next chapter, philanthropy has long been considered conducive to happiness and self-fulfillment, especially when the philanthropic acts are effectively, successfully, beneficial. Even beyond that, as we shall note in Chapter IV, there is a growing body of research suggesting that being philanthropic is conducive not just to higher self-esteem, or self-respect, but to worldly success—philanthropists tend to be and to be regarded as leaders, and to be materially successful. Thus it is an indisputable fact that being philanthropic is good for the benefactor as well as the beneficiary, and—here is the point—this combination is in the public interest.

3. Quality of Life

The "quality of life" focused on, accordingly, is that of **both** benefactors and beneficiaries, as well as that of the *civis,* or community, at all levels, even cosmopolitan.

As to beneficiaries, the quality-of-life benefit is obvious and straightforward, and the key is that it is not just decorative or "nice," but is actually, precisely, empowering—beginning with supplying urgent material needs (food, clothing, shelter, employment, etc.), and graduating to cultural or environmental needs, advantages, and enhancements.

Benefactors benefit by developing themselves—growing in their humanity or humaneness, more so as the constancy and intensity or depth of their engagement in philanthropy increases. For donors and volunteers, philanthropy is ennobling—in their own eyes, in the respect of witnesses, and objectively, because privately and personally assuming public or civic responsibilities is in itself beneficial. Eighteenth-century Enlightenment thinkers (see Chapter II) followed the Classical tradition in considering happiness a fundamental value to be sought, and that doing good for others is a sure way to achieve it. In this tradition, happiness in benefaction is regarded as evidence that philanthropy is ordained in Natural Law—our happiness as benefactors is how we know and can be sure that our philanthropy "follows the *Logos*" and is in harmony with the *Logos.* Modern physiological research has indicated that doing good activates pleasure centers in the brain, making us feel good when we do good; and again, sociological research has suggested to some that philanthropic activity is conducive to worldly success.

So let it be said: benefactors—yes, "do-gooders"—constitute one of the best—most productive and edifying—traditions in human history. From generation to generation, down through the ages, in all cultures, the individuals and groups are worth identifying as such, who out of consideration for others, have had the private initiative to assume public or civic responsibilities, by addressing and trying to solve public problems, even trying to improve the human condition. Their philanthropy defines who they were and are—what kind of people. Those with philanthropic character are the best. They define what kind of world they want, and actually work to help create it—an intrinsically optimistic enterprise, predicated on an ability and willingness to see into the future, and to try helping to improve it.

By adding "quality of life" to our definition, we aim to enhance philanthropy's appeal; whereas very few people today care about philanthropy as such (much less, know what it is and means), all surveys indicate that everyone's top priority is "quality of life." What we are saying is that philanthropy in the Classical tradition aims for it, and is a tried and true, often considered the best, way to achieve it.

This Classical humane idea of philanthropy may be especially appealing to the new generation of philanthropists today, who do not accept the Old Paradigm's (cf. Chapter III, below) rhetoric of "giving back" out of moral obligation, etc. The new donors are younger, still parenting, looking for meaning in their lives and ways to inculcate and cultivate values in their privileged children. They want, and in fact need, a constructive approach to philanthropy, as a value-intense continuation of their investment portfolios—investing in a better world, in "making a difference," in quality, and not just quantity, of life. As philanthropy today moves beyond being *chic*, to becoming at least potentially a popular movement, the Classical humane concept of philanthropy is well-suited for building philanthropy into one's life-style as more than decoration—as actually integral and integrating to the whole (cf. Chapter IV).

II. Philanthropy's Finest Hour: the American Revolution

A. Introduction

We have noted that few practitioners in "philanthropy" today care very much how the word is defined, and that what we have called the "Classical" humanistic or humane concept of philanthropy, based on its original coinage in *Prometheus Bound*, has a clear and inspiring meaning and tradition which can be stated in modern terms as, "private initiatives for public good, focusing on quality of life."

So—what? Does any of this matter? This chapter offers a case in point. American historians, through no particular fault of their own, have not known that "private initiatives for public good, focusing on quality of life" might be a subject for historical study. If, for example, "philanthropy" is defined as "rich people helping poor people," it is then a subject that is marginal at best in American historiography—nice, decorative, perfectly respectable, but relatively trivial to the main lines of interpretation of our national development and experience. If, on the other hand, "private initiatives for public good, focusing on quality of life" is an objective phenomenon, it can be studied, especially when it is institutionalized—a subject of historical analysis paralleling the histories of government and of the economy, the other two sectors. In that case, it suggests a reconsideration of our national history—not least because ours is the first modern democracy, a form of government in which philanthropy plays a leading role. "Democratic and philanthropic" springs to life as a subject for historical review.

In this chapter, to exemplify the potential fruits of such a review, we shall focus on the American Revolution and the founding of our national government. This will not be a history of those events, but rather an analysis of their philanthropic content and its significance. The Revolutionary period was certainly a time, and perhaps the only one so far, when America had a leading culture that might be called "philanthropic." A hardy perennial question for historians and others ever since has been, What made our Founding Fathers so extraordinarily gifted and high-minded in their great work together? The answer we propose is: their philanthropy, in the Classical mode. If this is so, it has instructional and edifying value for us today—it means that we already have an example to learn from, not just of individual heroic American philanthropist role-models, but of what a philanthropic culture might be and do for our national history.

Political revolutions—in R.R. Palmer's classic phrase "unconstitutional changes in the constitution of a polity"—are by definition political, but are not governmental until they succeed. Reform movements of any kind almost always begin as philanthropy, with "voluntary associations," as they have been called, of public-spirited, civic, individuals—with, that is, the private assumption of public or civic responsibilities.

If we think of the American Revolution as democratic politics, in which the closest analogy we know is how politics works today in our democracy, with political parties and an existing form of government assumed, we cannot understand pre-Revolutionary America. A closer analogy to pre-Revolutionary politics is common philanthropic practice, in which private persons raise private voluntary contributions of "time, talent, and treasure" in new associations, to address and try to solve civic problems.

The American Revolution more closely resembled traditional philanthropic practice than it did traditional political practice—indeed, one might even say that what was revolutionary about it was precisely the application of philanthropic, "voluntary association" routines to nation-building and national politics. In the American Revolution, the "unconstitutional change" was the application of philanthropic customs, values and practices to government.

B. The Case in Point

Alexander Hamilton, in the opening paragraph of the very first *Federalist Paper*, launched the Founders' advocacy for the ratification of our Constitution with these words:

"It has been frequently remarked that it seems to have been reserved to the people of this country, by their conduct and example, to decide the important question, whether societies of men are really capable or not of establishing good government from reflection and choice, or whether they are forever destined to depend for their political constitutions on accident and force. If there be any truth in the remark, the crisis at which we are arrived may with propriety be regarded as the era in which that decision is to be made; and a wrong election of the part we shall act may, in this view, deserve to be considered as the general misfortune of mankind.

This idea will add the **inducements of philanthropy** to those of patriotism, to heighten the solicitude which all considerate and **good men** must feel for the event. **Happy** will it be if our choice should be directed by a judicious estimate of our true interests, **unperplexed and unbiased by considerations not connected with the public good.**" [Emphases mine.]

First, it is safe to say that Hamilton's use of the word "philanthropy" in this extremely important instance, has generally gone unnoticed, or at least un-appreciated, by both historians and philanthropists, who tend to gloss over it in part because they do not recognize it—they have no clear or pertinent definition of the term already in their own minds. Hamilton, however, was choosing his words quite carefully, and it is clear from its context that his understanding of the word falls squarely within the Classical tradition.

Hamilton was not unique, in this understanding, among his contempo-raries—as he says, "It has been frequently remarked…"—and indeed there are countless other examples, of which three, quite diverse, may suffice to be cited here. In 1776, Thomas Paine had written in *Common Sense*, his very popular and influential tract for independence:

"The cause of America is in a great measure the cause of all mankind. Many circumstances have, and will arise, which are not local, but universal, and through which the principles of all **Lovers of Man-kind** are affected, and in the Event of which, their Affections are interested." [Emphasis mine.]

Benjamin Franklin, who as we shall see was and is still today America's paragon of Classical philanthropy, wrote during the Revolution: "**We are fighting for the dignity and happiness of human nature.**" [Emphasis mine—we shall recall these words below.]

George Washington, the Father of our Country, Commanding General of the Revolutionary Army (serving *pro bono*) and first President of the United States, and a man who chose words carefully, often signed his letters "Philanthropically yours,".

Historians generally understand that these and the innumerable similar expressions were clichés of the 18th-century European Enlightenment, exemplifying its influence in America. What is generally not appreciated is the importance of Classical *philanthropia* in both the Enlightenment itself, and especially in the American Enlightenment—and perforce, the American Revolution, arguably the Enlightenment's most powerful expression. Standard histories of this period do not use the word "philanthropy" or its cognates; but if those works are read with this Classical definition in mind, the phenomenon of philanthropy jumps out all over the place—it is revealed having been not just common, but a leading influence on the actual history of the period.

In this chapter, therefore, we shall attempt to illuminate the significance of philanthropy's appearance in the first *Federalist*. We shall propose that philanthropy as Classically conceived was a fundamental cause or conducive condition of, and influence upon, the American Revolution and the birth of our nation. Finally, we shall suggest in this and succeeding chapters, how and why this might matter to practical American philanthropy today and tomorrow.

C. The Renaissance of the Word and Idea

For over a thousand years, the Classical view of philanthropy lay buried in forgotten manuscripts in Western Christendom's monastic libraries. Medieval Christianity focused on issues of salvation, worship, and ecclesiastical administration. The economy did not even begin to recover until the tenth century, and then only very slowly, so that poor relief and Christian charity were the most common expressions of the broader phenomenon of practical philanthropy. Benefactors did it to seek salvation from their sins, and as a form of worship. The "love of what it is to be human" was of no conscious concern. Philosophy was neglected in favor of theology, and education was reduced to professional training for the clergy or monastic life. The few who were literate felt no need nor use for "pagan" or "secular" texts. Since in any case all books had to be laboriously copied by hand, the few produced were higher-priority religious books. Classical Greek was for all practical purposes a dead language in the West; even Latin had deteriorated to the point that when Classical authors began to be recovered in the twelfth century (often from Arabic sources), special training and linguistic expertise were required to read and understand them. For secular purposes, it was not until Italian Renaissance of the 14th–15th centuries, and the Northern Renaissance in the 16th, that recently developed urban conditions invoked Classical culture as once again interesting and useful, so that Western Civilization as a whole could be "reborn."

When that happened, the recovery of Classical language, thought, learning, and art was exciting, exhilarating, inspiring and invigorating, with revolutionary transformations in many fields of thought and endeavor. But the recovery itself was slow and hard work until the late fifteenth century, when the printing press stimulated an explosion of publishing, just in time to empower, in the sixteenth century, both the Reformation in religion and the Scientific Revolution.

One result of the vast recovery of Classical culture and civic humanism, was that the word and concept of "philanthropy" was recovered, revived, and translated into vernacular languages. On the scholarly side Sir Francis Bacon in 1592 had written that his "vast contemplative ends" were a product of his *philanthropia*," and on the practical side in his 1608 essay "On Goodness," he defined it as "the affecting of the weale of men... what the Grecians call *philanthropia*." This in itself is remarkable—that "philanthropy" was introduced into English as a full **synonym** for both active and contemplative "goodness." Also following the Classical concept was the first English Dictionary of 1623, in which its editor Henry Cockeram cited "philanthropy" as a synonym for "humanitie" (in Latin, *humanitas*)—thus reaffirming the full-Classical formulation.

This was a very strong start for a new word in English, to be adopted by two leading authorities as synonymous of both active and contemplative "goodness" and "humanitie"—the more so because "humanity" was a loaded term in the Renaissance. Though the cultural "rebirth" had begun in Italy well before it arose in transalpine countries, its spread was both wide and deep, in what is still referred to as the "Northern" Renaissance. The Classical tradition of liberal education, in both ancient (Latin and Greek) and vernacular languages, was the cutting edge of thorough cultural transformation. Northern "Humanism" was more intensely religious than its Italian predecessor; "Christian Humanism"—i.e., the recovery and study of ancient texts of Christianity, and especially retranslations of the Bible into vernacular languages—was a leading cause of the Reformation. In the North as well as in Italy and ancient times, the fullest development of *humanitas* was the goal of education in "the good arts," the "liberal arts," or the "studies of humanity"—*studia humanitatis*—or simply the "humanities." Accordingly *humanitas*, or *philanthropia*—the love of humanity—was the epitome, result, and goal, of liberal education.

It is notable that in both the Italian and Northern Renaissances, this sort of "humanitie" was as a practical matter also associated with freedom and democracy against tyranny, as it had been in ancient Greece. The Renaissance itself was launched in Florence at the turn of the 15th century as a movement of what modern scholars have called "civic humanism," when the Florentine Republic's citizens successfully defended themselves in 1402 against the tyrannical Giangaleazzo Visconti, Duke of Milan, just as the citizens of republican Athens had against the Persian kings in ancient Greece. In rallying the people and celebrating the victory, Florentine humanist statesmen referred to the heroes, ideas, values, and even artistic and rhetorical styles of Classical urban culture in the Roman Republic and Periclean Athens—models they could not find in the Bible or medieval cultural history. In the North, Christian humanism's role in the Reformation was also considered a liberating, empowering, and in some systems of Protestant church government, democratizing, influence.

D. The Seed Finds Fertile Ground in America

The translation of *philanthropia* into English in the early 17th century was especially propitious, because this was precisely the moment when English settlers came to America, seeking to be free, to be saved, and to create a good society. What happened here was that philanthropy itself was also liberated, to develop its fullest and deepest historical expression. In America, humanity and philanthropy together took a new turn.

1. The Necessity of Voluntary Associations
At the practical level, these 17th-century colonists found themselves in a new and unique place in history: they brought their civilization to a wilderness, where they had no choice but to create a new way of life. Here was a "blank slate" if ever there was one, a kind of Robinson Crusoe situation.

What is more, anything and everything that was done, they had to do themselves. In the Old World, what we today think of as public administration was the responsibility of traditional established powers—the church, secular government, and the landed aristocracy. But in the New World, there were no such powers on which to rely. Therefore every problem the colonials met, individually or collectively, had to be solved by the people themselves, individually or collectively. In Classical terms, if any *res publica*—"public thing"—needed doing, either the settlers did it themselves, for themselves, voluntarily, or it was left undone.

Another constraint was their almost total lack of liquidity—they had no cash. In any case, because land was plentiful and cheap, paid labor was scarce and dear. Lacking money to pay for labor that was in any case expensive, they created alternatives: an indenture system (industrial-scale slavery came later), an elaborate barter economy, and for large private and civic projects, reliance on cooperation and collaboration. Institutionalized "voluntary associations" arose, of every imaginable kind and description—to an extent later noticed by Alexis de Tocqueville as distinctively American.

One of the first of these, if not the first, was the *Mayflower* Compact itself of 1620, entered into on shipboard while the Pilgrims were still offshore, but in American waters, as it were. The signers "solemnly and mutually, in the Presence of God and one another, combine ourselves together into a civil Body Politick, for our better Ordering and Preservation." Thus one of the first American governments was itself a voluntary association. The first corporation in America was also a voluntary association in the Massachusetts Bay Colony, created to train young men for the clergy: Harvard College (1636). Both these examples were, please note, "private initiatives for public good, focusing on quality of life."

In sum, the English colonists found themselves in a new and unique historical situation, requiring innovation and collaboration, often through voluntary associations. In everything from barn-raising, road-building, defense, and fire-fighting, to founding schools and colleges, hospitals and orphanages, philosophical societies and libraries, new churches and even new religions—Americans learned to create their own personal and civic "quality of life" through "private initiatives for public good, focusing on quality of life."

2. The Commonwealth Ideal

It was important that from the outset, these communities and their ways of life had extraordinary value-intensity. They were seeking to create **good** societies. In fact, they already had a value-intensive word for a *res publica* in which all citizens worked together to create a good society: "commonwealth," or "common weale." As with so many other good words in modern times, "commonwealth" has lost its original clarity; it came from the Latin *cum* (with) + *munus* (service) and the Middle English *wele* or Anglo-Saxon *wela* meaning well-being or prosperity. Combining all those roots, the word meant general well-being, common good, or more precisely something like: general prosperity through mutual service.

Three of the earliest and leading English colonies—Massachusetts, Virginia, and Pennsylvania—were designated "Commonwealths." England itself was called a "Commonwealth" under the Puritan Protectorate of Oliver Cromwell, 1649-1660. In England the word and its moralistic idea had achieved common usage with the early 16th-century socially critical "Commonwealth Movement," which stressed poor-relief based on Christian moral values—Sir (St.) Thomas More was said to be a "Commonwealthman"; his *Utopia* (1515) went far in this direction, exemplifying in a secular community traditional monastic ideals of Christian communism.

The concept's values were understood as embodying objective natural laws. The core assumption was the Classical notion that just as all members of a living body are mutually interdependent, each with its own function serving the well-being of the whole body, and unable to exist otherwise, so also, all members of a body politic are and should be mutually interdependent and inseparable, literally unable to exist in isolation. As a Classical (Stoic) idea, it was revived in Renaissance political thought and particularly in England, familiar to us from Shakespeare and John Donne's often-quoted *Meditation XVII* (1624): "No man is an island, entire of itself, every man is a piece of the continent, a part of the main..."

It follows in this context that the basic social sin, the root of all social evil, was thought to be greed, or covetousness. Differences in wealth were considered necessary for the good of the whole, but with wealth came social responsibility. The wealth acquired by the fortunate few had existed before them, and would continue to exist after them, in other hands; they were only its temporary custodians or stewards. What they did with that wealth would define their individual characters and the qualities of their lives, and their ultimate judgment and reputation. English Puritans under Cromwell, as well as Puritan and Quaker settlers in the New World, hoped to create ideal communities based on these values. Philanthropy and charity were intended by them to be the norm here in America.

One of the chief promoters of this Puritan, Classical, practical, tradition was the preacher Cotton Mather, who as late as 1710 published a widely-read American classic, *Bonifacius, or an Essay to Do Good*. Mather seems to have been concerned at this late date about the erosion of the original ideals, against which he advocated philanthropic benefaction as a way of life. Though his context was Christian, his idea was also characteristically American and explicitly Classical, on the threshold of the Enlightenment.

> Let no man pretend to the Name of *A Christian*, who does not Approve the proposal of *A Perpetual Endeavour to Do Good in the World*. What pretension can Such a man have to be *A Follower of the Good One?* The Primitive *Christians* gladly accepted and improved the Name, when the Pagans by a mistake Styled them, *Chrestians*; Because it Signifyed, *Useful Ones*. The *Christians* who have no Ambition to be So, Shall be condemned by the Pagans; among whom it was a Term of the Highest Honour, to be termed, *A Benefactor;* to have *Done Good,* was accounted *Honourable*. The Philosopher [i.e., Aristotle], being asked why Every one desired so much to look upon a Fair Object! He answered That it *was a Question of a Blind man.* If any man ask, as wanting the Sense of it, What is it worth the while to *Do Good* in the world! I must Say, *It Sounds not like the Question of a Good man."* (p.21)

Mather argued, in the Stoic tradition, that "Humanity" (i.e., in the Classical sense of *humanitas*, or humane-ness, which contained the notion of goodness) "teaches us to take Notice of all that are our Kindred. Nature bespeaks, that which we call a *Natural Affection* to all that are *Akin* to us." (72) Mather's many practical suggestions for doing good had strong civic emphases—founding schools, libraries, hospitals, useful publications, etc. They were not primarily about rich people helping poor people, but about private initiatives for public good, focusing on quality of life.

E. To Which Was Added: The Scottish Enlightenment

At roughly the same time, another link was being forged that also connected the Classical concept of philanthropy to the American Revolution: the European, and especially Scottish, Enlightenment. Here too, if one reads standard histories with the idea of Classical philanthropy in mind, one discovers it everywhere.

Arthur Herman, in *How the Scots Invented the Modern World,* has pointed out that in 1770 there were about 200,000 Scots in America—8% of the total Colonial population of 2.5 million. Yet one-third (19 out of 56) of the signers of the *Declaration of Independence* were Scottish or Scots-Irish; perhaps half of the troops with Washington at Valley Forge were Ulster Scots. Whereas Highland Scots tended to be Tory, Lowland (e.g., Glasgow) Scots and Ulster Scotch-Irish were overwhelmingly Patriots, in much larger numbers. A Hessian officer in the Revolution who brought an Old-World perspective to it and clearly didn't "get it" about humankind as a whole, is often quoted as having written, "Call this war by whatever name you may, only call it not an American rebellion; it is nothing more or less than a Scotch Irish Presbyterian Rebellion."

How was it that the Scots became so active and influential in the Revolution?

First, Scotland already had strong democratic inclinations. The Scottish Presbyterian Church was the most democratic national institution in Europe, organized around representative regional synods which were represented in a national General Assembly. One of that Church's founders, a Moderator of the General Assembly, was George Buchanan, a 16th-century humanist familiar with both Classical and Christian thought, who as early as 1579 in a treatise on *The Law of Government Among the Scots* had advocated popular sovereignty for secular governments.

Second, the Scottish Church had, since the Reformation, energetically promoted lay education so that people could read the Scriptures in English. As a result, by the 18th century Scotland had become the most literate country in Europe—over half of its citizens could read and write. This of course encouraged broad intellectual activity; by 1750 every town had a lending library, over half of the books circulated were secular, and many borrowers were tradesmen. Scottish universities were also renowned as excellent, drawing students from all over Europe.

Third, in this bracing philanthropic and democratic atmosphere, "voluntary associations" abounded, promoting progress. The Advocates Library in Edinburgh was a principal resource nourishing Enlightenment thought, as was the Society for Encouraging Arts, Sciences, Manufactures and Agriculture. In Glasgow Robert Foulis, a self-taught bookseller and printer like Ben Franklin in Philadelphia, promoted initiatives to unite the practical, intellectual and artistic trades in a freely cross-fertilizing civic culture. He established a School for the Arts of Design that, like his own printing press, became part of the University of Glasgow. Glasgow merchants formed a Literary Society, a Sacred Music Institution, and a Hodge Podge Club that invited leading intellectuals like Adam Smith to speak on current issues. Foulis was following the Classical Greek "paideian" ideal of community or society, which in all the parts are educational, promoting civilization or humane self-development. In 1768 the first volume of the *Encyclopaedia* (from *encyclos* = universal, and *paideia* = learning or culture) *Brittanica* was published in Edinburgh, purporting to portray all knowledge—practical, scientific, technological, and humane, as a coherent whole reflecting a coherent world.

Fourth, Scottish thinkers were progressive in exploring secular scientific grounds for values. The seventeenth-century Wars of Religion had undermined the authority, reliability, and stabilizing influence of both churches and governments as sources of values; religion in particular had become a source of disorder and oppression, rather than of order, in society and culture. Under increasing demand for order, both churches and states had hardened their positions into "absolutist" forms. But the Scientific Revolution from the 16th to the 18th centuries had reformulated many fundamental issues apart from religion, to be safe, and established mathematics and experimentation as preferred methods of inquiry and verification. Scholars and philosophers responded accordingly, and tried to create new systems of thought, grounded either in ideas they thought were certainly or self-evidently true, or in empirical evidence, or in logical connections between the two. None of these however gained supremacy as a universal system, universally accepted. Western civilization was disintegrating, into modern fragmented secularity—in which we address the world in separate parts, rather than as a coherent whole.

In all this intellectual ferment, a few Scottish philosophers explicitly embraced the Classical view of philanthropy as a ground for values, and their work influenced the American Revolution.

1. Anthony Ashley Cooper, Third Earl of Shaftesbury (1671-1713)

Shaftesbury was a student of John Locke's (who in 1679 had organized a voluntary association of scholars called the "Philanthropoy"), and a prolific moral philosopher who espoused the Classical concept of philanthropy as a philosophy of life. He believed that the virtuous person strives to develop an "equal, just and universal friendship" with all humanity, and that to be virtuous is to promote the good of all mankind. His motto was "Love, Serve." He believed that loving and serving others develops our full humanity, that we enjoy doing so, and that our enjoyment is evidence that doing good is in harmony with Natural Law (cf. the Classical *Logos*)—all of which explains why we do good at all. Helping others fills us with a sense of well-being and pleasure; *being* good means *doing* good, which causes *feeling* good—an harmonious life, in harmony with the *cosmos* (which contained the notion of, and embodied, the *Logos*).

Through Natural Law, this doctrine of philanthropy extended readily into politics, as it had for the Greeks, in their tag "philanthropic and democratic." Shaftesbury compared human civilization with the "polishing" of gems, which produced in civil society a certain "politeness" (etymologically, the condition of being polished). This "politeness" toward others, he thought, is nourished by liberty. "All politeness is owing to Liberty....We polish one another, and rub off our Corners and rough Sides by a sort of amicable Collision. To restrain this is inevitably to bring a Rust upon Men's Under-standing. 'Tis a destroying of Civility, Good Breeding, and even Charity itself...."

2. Francis Hutcheson (1694-1746)
Another Scot and follower of Shaftesbury, Francis Hutcheson (1694-1746), dedicated in homage to Shaftesbury in 1725 an *Inquiry into the Original of Our Ideas of Beauty and Virtue*. In 1726 Hutcheson wrote, in his *Essay on the Nature and Conduct of the Passions and Affections*: "From the very frame of our nature we are determined to perceive pleasure in the practice of virtue, and to approve of it when practiced by ourselves or others."

Love is our most important feeling; love for others is the starting point of all morality. "There is no mortal without some love towards others, and desire in the happiness of some other persons as well as his own." A benevolent "fellow-feeling" and "delight in the Good of others" gives us our sense of right and wrong. We know that what is beneficial to someone we love is good, because it gives us pleasure to contemplate it; we know that what hurts another person is bad, because it pains us to see his unhappiness. We all want benevolence and benefaction to others because they produce "happiness."

"*Happiness*" was a key word and concept in the Enlightenment. Garry Wills' study of the Declaration of Independence, *Inventing America* (see App. III) is especially clear and strong on this point, though he did not mention its connection to Stoic philosophy. Etymologically, the word derives from the same root as "happen," and signifies not just an event, but a fitting event—

an event that is suitable to, connects with, is appropriate to or in harmony with, its circumstance. When that "happens," we feel pleasure; when we are in a "mishap," we feel pain or stress. The goodness we feel when things fit smoothly together, humming along, is evidence of harmony with the *Logos*. That is why the "pursuit of happiness" is asserted in the *Declaration*, as a "self-evident" truth, to be an "inalienable right" of all humanity, right up there with life and liberty. We all have an inalienable right, grounded in our human nature, to pursue happiness, *kata Logos*.

In other words, philanthropy—doing good, loving humanity—is the ground of ethical values, in accordance with Natural Law. Our consciences necessarily cultivate an altruistic benevolence and affection for our fellowmen, and these universal laws of morality are continuous with those of natural science—extending into ethics the coherence scientists find in physics.

Here again there were political implications. Hutcheson extended this line of reasoning, also as an expression of Natural Law, to Natural Rights.

Liberty, he said, is a fundamental human right—universal, and belonging to all humans everywhere. "As nature has implanted in every man a desire of his own happiness, and many tender affections towards others...and granted to each one some understanding and active powers with a natural impulse to exercise them for the purposes of those affections; 'tis plain each one has a natural right to exert his power according to his own judgement and inclination, for these purposes...."

3. Extension to the American Revolution
From there it was only a short step to the political theory of the American Revolution. **Thomas Reid**, a professor at the Universities of Aberdeen and Glasgow, promoted what he called a philosophy of "common sense," grounded in "self-evident" truths—"no sooner understood than they are believed, because they carry the light of truth in itself." Thomas Paine adopted Reid's phrase *Common Sense* as the title of his pro-Revolution tract, at the suggestion of **Benjamin Rush** of Philadelphia, a medical doctor who had studied in Scotland. Rush was a close friend of Benjamin Franklin, who co-founded with him the American Philosophical Society.

A major intellectual influence on the Revolution was **John Witherspoon**. a Scot who became president of Princeton College and modelled it after the University of Edinburgh. He was the most influential promoter of the idea that the Revolution was God's work, and he influenced Hamilton's

First *Federalist Paper.* "It has often been said that the present is likely to be an important era to America. I think we may safely say, it is likely to be an important era in the history of mankind." "We have the opportunity of forming plans of government upon the most rational, just, and equal principles." He noted that this had never before happened in history, and if it failed, the opportunity might never happen again.

Where the Scottish scholar **Adam Ferguson,** in his *Essay on the History of Civil Society* (1768), had used the words "civilization" and "civil society" in the Classical sense of meaning that they promote full humanity, John Witherspoon wrote, "I do expect (from the success of the Revolution) a progress as in every other human art, so in the order and perfection of human society." Just as in *Prometheus Bound,* "all the arts that mortals have come from Prometheus," so the philanthropic and democratic new nation in America would nourish and further enhance all arts. The Classical Greek, and natural, association of "philanthropic and democratic" was fully revived, and ready for practical implementation.

F. Ben Franklin: the Revolution's "Necessary Man," and Paragon of American Philanthropy

These conducive conditions—the Classical, humanistic, idealistic concept of philanthropy, together with the practical constraints in Colonial America that necessitated reliance on voluntary associations for achieving quality of life, meditated through the Scottish Enlightenment which explicitly influenced American Revolutionary thought—coincided in Benjamin Franklin (1706-1790), who has been called the American Revolution's "Necessary Man," and who was and is, in thought and practice, the Paragon of American Philanthropy.

If today we seek a leading role-model for philanthropy, Franklin offers an excellent example of an intentionally philanthropic life-style. Widely regarded in his own time and ours as "the first great American," lionized throughout 18th-century Europe and America as a model of American values, and especially of the Enlightenment in America, he self-consciously and purposefully built his life around a distinctive American version of the "private assumption of public responsibilities," which is the essence of the Classical Greek "philanthropic and democratic" ideal. Even his political rival in France, John Adams, avowed that "there was scarcely a peasant or citizen" who "did not consider him as a friend to humankind." With elegant and powerful concision Immanuel Kant, the greatest philosopher of the

German Enlightenment, who certainly knew what he was talking about, called Franklin the "new Prometheus" for stealing fire from the heavens in his scientific experiments with lightning as electricity.

Franklin himself had strong connections with the Scottish Enlightenment; he was called "Dr. Franklin" because he had been awarded honorary degrees from all three main Scottish Universities: St. Andrews, Glasgow and Edinburgh. While travelling there he had met and personally befriended the leading Scottish Enlightenment thinkers; he said as he left in 1759, "I believe Scotland would be the country I should choose to spend the remainder of my days in." As he later told the French about the American Revolution: "We are fighting for the dignity and happiness of human nature." He advised Jefferson to use Thomas Reid's phrase, "self-evident" in the Declaration of Independence in the assertion:

> "We hold these Truths to be Self-Evident: that All Men are Created Equal, that they are endowed by their Creator with certain inalienable Rights, that among these are Life, Liberty, and the Pursuit of Happiness."

So the "pursuit of happiness," as a "self-evident," God-given, and thus inalienable, human right, which our Founding Fathers understood from the Scottish Enlightenment especially as the natural result of doing good for one's fellow humans, or philanthropy in the Classical mode, informed the idealism of the American Revolution. Thus were the "inducements of philanthropy," as Hamilton put it, added to those of patriotism and enshrined in our predicating documents as a nation.

Franklin himself said that if his life was useful to his country, it was owing to Cotton Mather's book, *Bonifacius: or An Essay to Do Good*. What must precocious young Ben Franklin have thought when he read, "It is possible the Wisdom of a Poor man may Start a Proposal, that may Save a City, [even] Serve a Nation!" (31)

Mather's book seems to have been among the inspirations of Franklin's first published work in 1722, when he was only 16—a series of 14 letters to his brother's Boston newspaper, the *Courant*, submitted in the disguise of a middle-aged widow, "Silence Dogood." In these "Dogood Papers" he proposed, among other private initiatives for public good, focusing on quality of life: a voluntary association of married persons to provide insurance for widows and spinsters; the separation of church and state; and promoting "the rights and liberties of my country," as opposed to "arbitrary government and unlimited power." Franklin soon declared his own independence (from apprenticeship to his brother and other constraints in Boston), by escaping to New York, then London, and finally to Philadelphia. By 1726 he was a printer there in his own right.

In Philadelphia (*n.b.* the Classical humanistic influence: *philos adelphos*—brotherly love) he created perhaps the first American personal and intentional **system** of civic philanthropy. In 1727, when he was only 21, he formed a voluntary association, the famous "Junto": 12 tradesmen and artisans like himself, who met on Friday evenings to discuss current issues and events—a civic discussion. There were four qualifications for membership, of which the second was the "love [of] mankind in general" (i.e., "philanthropy"); the others were: respect for other members, religious and philosophical toleration, and love and pursuit of truth. Two years later (1729) he founded his own newspaper, the *Philadelphia Gazette*, and for the next thirty years he used the Junto as a sort of think-tank to generate and vet philanthropic ideas, together with the *Gazette* to mobilize public support, recruit volunteers, and solicit donations to implement them. This system was phenomenally productive and beneficial; among its results were: America's first subscription library (1731), a volunteer fire association, a fire insurance association, the American Philosophical (*philos sophia*—love of wisdom) Society (1743-4), an "academy" (1750—which became the University of Pennsylvania), a hospital (1752—with private donations stimulated by a challenge grant), the paving and patrolling of public streets through private donations, the finance and construction of a civic meeting house, and many others.

One of these merits special attention: in 1747 the Pennsylvania Colony was violently disrupted by Indians in the west, and French Canadian privateering in the lower Delaware River. The government in Philadelphia was Quaker, hence pacifist, and would do nothing. Franklin, increasingly frustrated with this inaction, consulted his Junto, and published a wake-up call in a pamphlet, *Plain Truth,* declaring that Pennsylvania was defenseless unless the people would take matters into their own hands. He proposed a "military association" to raise funds and a private militia; convened a meeting of tradesmen and mechanics, and with their approval called a larger meeting (in the hall which he had caused to be built with private donations for civic purposes). There he presented a "pledge" for people to sign, organizing themselves into a "Militia Association," featuring self-supporting democratically (n.b.) administered military companies with elected representatives from each county to a "General Military Council" whose regulations would "have the Force of LAWS with us." Immediately 1,000 volunteers signed up, and within a few weeks Franklin had recruited more than a hundred companies with over 10,000 men-at-arms, for which he raised over £6,500 in a public lottery.

This philanthropic project was a prototype of the American Revolution. What is more, both Franklin himself and Thomas Penn (the Proprietor William Penn's son, in England) recognized its ominous potency. Franklin took pains to lower his own profile in the venture, and to restrain the new military association from unnecessary gestures of opposition to the government; Penn wrote that this Franklin was a very dangerous man, that what he had accomplished was "little less than Treason." If the people of Pennsylvania could act "independent of this Government, why should they not Act against it?"

Why not, indeed? Penn and Franklin were of course right. After 150 years' experience and schooling, as it were, in the practice of philanthropy private initiatives for public good, focusing on quality of life in all areas of the Colonists' civic interest, it gradually dawned on them that perhaps they could also have the kind of government they wanted—that the same methods and skills which were routine in their voluntary associations, could also be applied to politics and government—in fact, instituting and constituting democratic self-government. From the Mayflower Compact, through Franklin's private army, to the American Revolution, was only the unfolding of practical logic.

So when the British rule became increasingly abrasive and obnoxious in the 1760s and '70s, the tools of independent resistance were already at hand. The great conspirator Sam Adams issued a public call for "voluntary associations" to be established throughout the colonies, to advocate and prepare for independence. The "Sons of Liberty" and Committees of Correspondence were the readily forthcoming response. The Classical tag, "philanthropic and democratic," was turning out to be true—philanthropy, by promoting the desire, and training the skills, of citizenship, and especially the arts of democratic compromise to get things done peacefully through conflict resolution, the habitual private assumption of public responsibilities, was our school for democracy, in how to accomplish the American Revolution.

Ben Franklin has been called the American Revolution's "necessary man," second only to George Washington, and the only one of the Founding Fathers who helped shape all five, and signed four, of our nation's founding documents: the Albany Plan of Union, the Declaration of Independence, the treaty of alliance with France, the Peace treaty with England, and the Constitution itself. In the Revolution Franklin was ubiquitous, though always in the background, as the elder advisor to others playing more conspicuous roles. Only seven years after his private army was raised, he was the first to propose a federal system of government, in his Albany Plan of 1754, wherein power would be shared between both a national government and separate state governments; his Articles of Confederation in 1775 more closely approximated the final Constitution than did the official Articles of 1787. Much of this work was done as a private citizen volunteer, rather than in any official government employment. He considered his work as a Founding Father to be part and parcel of his "doing good" philosophy—loving wisdom by loving mankind. For all these reasons, Franklin personifies the American Revolution as philanthropy—the application of standard philanthropic practice to nation-building. And yet, the word "philanthropy" does not appear in the indices, nor in the texts at least that I could find, of the four currently leading tricentennial biographies of Franklin, by leading American historians. Again, this is not their fault—the subject has not been properly taught by its profession.

3. Paul Revere, et al.

Also without using the word "philanthropy," the American historian David Hackett Fischer has personified the phenomenon in *Paul Revere's Ride* (Oxford, 1994), in which he portrays Revere as a kind of grassroots version of Ben Franklin. Like Franklin, Revere was a son of Boston and a young reader of Cotton Mather, especially impressed by Mather's simile of having two oars in the water: one is a person's vocation in life as tradesman, artisan, or whatever; the other oar is following Christ's calling to do good work in the world; either oar alone will have us rowing in circles, whereas if we row through life with both oars we shall get to Heaven!

Fischer describes Revere as "an associating sort of man" (19)—a natural and prodigious joiner and networker in voluntary associations. In 1750, when he was fifteen, he formed an association, complete with mission statement, of seven boy bell-ringers in Boston's Old North Church. In 1760 at 25, he became a Mason, one of whose five commitments was "community service"; by 1770 at 35, he was Master of his Lodge. He helped found the Massachusetts Mutual Fire Insurance Company (as its first signator), and the Massachusetts Charitable Mechanic Association (as its first president). He helped arrange for streetlights in Boston and regulation of the Boston market. He joined the Caucus Club, one of three political associations in

Boston, and the Long Room Club, a secret and more selective one. In 1765 he joined the Sons of Liberty, who played a leading role in opposing the Stamp Act; he probably designed their silver seal and their silver punch bowl commemorating the "Glorious 92" members of the Massachusetts legislature who refused to rescind a Circular Letter sent to all the colonies urging (voluntary) united resistance to the Townshend Acts. In 1773-1775, he made at least five trips to New York and Philadelphia to help coordinate growing resistance to British impositions. Boston's "revolutionary movement," Fischer says, was an "open alliance of many different groups," (27) in which Revere's role was as networker and communicator. When he decided to prevent British repressions in 1774, "his chosen instrument was a favorite device in Boston: the voluntary association." As Revere himself later wrote, "in the Fall of 1774 and Winter of 1775, I was one of upwards of thirty, chiefly mechanics, who formed themselves (n.b.) into a committee for the purpose of watching the movements of the British soldiers....We held our meetings at the Green Dragon Tavern." Revere was its leader. (51) His famous "Ride" succeeded, Fischer says, because he had so well organized his voluntary association in advance.

When the occasion arrived, those who responded to it were also voluntary associations: the Minutemen, organized by towns, with prepared strategies of response to military threat—including, apparently, the remarkably wise strategic yet detailed order not to fire unless first fired upon by the British Regulars. Though volunteers, they were remarkably well-disciplined, and revolutionary in the sense that officers consulted their men before deciding what to do—unheard-of for warfare, routine for philanthropic voluntary associations such as Franklin's.

4. The Declaration of Independence

The Declaration of Independence presents the first instance in history in which the creation of a national government was formally preceded by a statement of idealistic purpose addressed to all humanity, on behalf of, and for the benefit of, all humanity. Where do you think they got that idea?

In the context of "the Laws of Nature and of Nature's God," the Declaration laid down in principle justifications not only for this rebellion but for all political rebellions anywhere, ever. After the case was made, the Declaration closed with a unique mix of governmental and private philanthropic language: first declaring themselves to be "Representatives" of the "united [sic] States of America," "appealing to the Supreme Judge of the world for the rectitude of our intentions, do, in the Name, and by the Authority of the good People of these Colonies" declare themselves free, sovereign and independent, and then: "we mutually pledge *to each other* our Lives, our Fortunes and our sacred Honor."

In other words, pretending to official status and on the authority of the People, they appeal to God for both salvation and protection, and nonetheless pledge **to each other**, their lives, fortunes and honor. Actually this was realistic, not histrionic or vain posturing; most of the 56 signers suffered heavily and personally as a result of this mutual covenant—five were captured by the British as traitors, tortured and killed; nine fought and died in the war; two lost their sons, another had two sons captured; and the homes of twelve were destroyed—all for their philanthropy. Perhaps philanthropy should have a martyrology, starting with Prometheus.

The American Revolution was thus conceived, planned, organized, funded, and implemented by private initiatives for public good, focusing on quality of life. Private donations funded it (with significant support from the French monarch—still a private entirety from its point of view—skillfully fundraised by Benjamin Franklin), and volunteers implemented it, explicitly as a philanthropic project—on behalf of, and for the good of, all humanity. Was this, or was it not, *philanthropia* in action?

5. The Constitution
We have already seen that the Constitution was explicitly framed by its leading advocates in the *Federalist Papers* as Classically philanthropic. The Constitutions "Preamble" was equally so—featuring private initiative, public good, and quality of life:

> "WE THE PEOPLE of the United States, in Order to form a more
> perfect Union, establish Justice, insure domestic Tranquility, provide
> for the common defence, promote the general Welfare, and secure
> the Blessings of Liberty to ourselves and our Posterity, do ordain and
> establish this Constitution for the United States of America."

We were also the first nation on Earth in which the people were the constituent power. The ratification process—in which private citizens assumed public responsibilities by personally and voluntarily promoting and voting to join the United States of America—was routine in philanthropy; all voluntary associations were and are formed and governed by their members.

We were also the first nation on Earth to declare that the purpose of its government was to provide for the people's quality of life. Quality of life had always been philanthropy's focus; now philanthropy was assigning it to government as well—explicitly philanthropic and democratic government, in the Classical tradition.

The very form of our national government was constructed on the model of voluntary associations. The first formal agreement by representatives of the Colonies to unify was called an "Association"—signed by members of the Continental Congress in Philadelphia on October 20, 1774. At every step of the way, the "members" of the association voluntarily declared their wish to join—in the case of the Confederation of course the members were by then the States (formerly Colonies). That formulation was succeeded by individual and collective People as members. The Constitution ensures that the civil contract is constantly renewed and sustained by checks and balances which protect and ensure the consent of the governed. The People—not the government as such—is collectively our sovereign power.

G. Conclusion

1. Summary
This chapter contains several theses, on two levels: within the chapter itself, and for this book as a whole.

a. In This Chapter
This chapter by itself presents four main ideas: **First**, that the American Revolution and the framing of our Constitution was, and was considered by the Founders, thoroughly and fundamentally "philanthropic," and in the Classical idealistic tradition. **Second**, that the Founders imbibed their philanthropic ideals and practices from two main sources: at the practical and institutional level, from 150 years' necessity and habit of accomplishing civic ends through voluntary associations; and philanthropically from the European, but particularly the Scottish, Enlightenment. **Third**, since the Scottish Enlightenment was clearly informed by Classical Stoicism and humanism, and since the Founding Fathers' ideas were clearly informed by the Scottish Enlightenment, the Scottish Enlightenment is a clear link connecting the Founders' philanthropic and political ideals with Classical Stoicism and humanism, which includes the Classical concept of philanthropy.

Fourth, these connections have not been noticed by either historians or philanthropists because they have not recognized them as philanthropy.

They have been accustomed to thinking of philanthropy vaguely, as "rich helping poor" or "advantaged helping disadvantaged," not to mention "giving" or "caring." These reductionist misconceptions have the effect of marginalizing and drastically undervaluing the true role and importance of philanthropy especially in America.

In other words, armed with the Classical humane view of philanthropy as "private initiatives for public good, focusing on quality of life"—practical idealism—we can see that building America and creating the United States was essentially philanthropic, evoked and strengthened practically as a matter of necessity in the Colonies; nourished and articulated idealistically in the European and particularly Scottish Enlightenment; both threads joining in the American Revolution. The Classical concept was explicitly and specifically understood as a defining influence by our Founding Fathers, who learned it from the Scottish Enlightenment, among other sources.

In sum, here in America, conceived as a purportedly philanthropic nation, Classical philanthropy reached its apotheosis, its noblest expression, which has effectually transformed the history of the modern world, for the purpose (as a regulative ideal, never achieved) of raising humanity to higher levels of civilization—squarely within the Promethean tradition!

The early history of the Republic, leading into the Jacksonian period, was one of rapid, tumultuous, growth and sorting-out of what had been accomplished. The onset of the Industrial Revolution, waves of immigration, urban development and westward expansion, together with shifting political practices and a new cast of characters in leadership positions, worked to dissolve the philanthropic culture and spirit of the Founding. The American Renaissance of literature in the 1830s, '40's and '50s, in the works of Hawthorne, Emerson, Thoreau, Melville and others, was essentially a protest against the perceived loss of Classical American values, and evidence that the flame of philanthropic, practical, idealism did not die with the Founders. In 1837, Ralph Waldo Emerson celebrated the philanthropic spirit of the Revolution in his "Concord Hymn," with his famous lines, "here once the embattled farmers stood/ And fired the shot heard 'round the world." In 1844, in his essay "The Young American," he wrote,

> "It seems so easy for America to inspire and express the most expansive and humane spirit; new-born, free, healthful, strong, the land of the laborer, of the democrat, of the philanthropist, of the believer, of the saint, she should speak for the human race. It is the country of the future."

b. For This Book

With reference to the book as a whole, this Chapter presents three main ideas:

> **First** (which might go without saying), is that carefully defining the word we use to name our profession makes a big difference. We have demonstrated this by applying it usefully to a subject of unquestionable significance: the American Revolution and the birth of our nation.

> **Second**, that one of the most respected periods in American history had a leading culture of philanthropy, and produced leading examples of philanthropists, who manifested philanthropic culture in their individual lives.

> **Third**, that defining "philanthropy" by reference to its etymology and original history may also be useful to modern philanthropic practice and understanding. It has the capacity to transform our customary, relatively vague and loose vocabulary, conceptualization, and rhetoric throughout our philanthropic practice—from fundraising and recruitment of volunteers, to civil and liberal education, to inculcating values in our children and practicing them ourselves, to strategizing about the future of the sector and its values in the world (see Chapter V, below).

This is a far more attractive vision for new and emerging donors; it can replace the dreary and negative litany of "giving away" and "giving back" to "non-profits," "exempt entities," and the "disadvantaged" in the "third" sector. In this view, philanthropy—developing and enhancing humanity— is not just constructive, about making a difference in the world through positive investments of time, talent, and treasure, but it is quintessentially American. Thus, if we may say so, with thanks to Hamilton, it adds "the inducements of patriotism" to those of philanthropy itself! Volunteers and donors may today stand in the great tradition of doing essentially what made this country great, and what may do so again, today and tomorrow.

2. Ramifications—Philanthropy and American History

Since the Revolution and ratification, our national history has also been more clearly informed by philanthropy, Classically conceived, than we generally appreciate. The philanthropic spirit of Colonial society-building travelled west with the frontier throughout the 19th century, continuing to be a practical necessity, and reinforcing the "philanthropic and democratic" development of the American character. All of private education and of religion in America have been necessarily philanthropic. Every reform movement in our history has begun as philanthropy—e.g., anti-slavery, women's suffrage, conservation, civil rights, feminism, peace, and environmentalism. All were "private initiatives for public good, focusing on quality of life," which speaks to the value of philanthropy to our national quality of life. Today most of our hospitals, almost all of our environmental and cultural institutions, and by far most human services agencies, are charitable corporations. Private citizens are the first to notice and respond to emerging public problems, and because they are free to do so in this philanthropic democracy, the charitable sector is our nation's early-warning system, our most sensitive perceptor of emerging challenges and opportunities in maintaining and achieving quality of life.

Philanthropy has also been the arena in which women have found their greatest fulfillment and influence. When careers in government and commerce were foreclosed to them, women have turned to philanthropy for free expression of their talents and resources, founding many of our major charitable organizations. Some commentators have used the problematic expression "community homemakers" to suggest that in philanthropy women's domestic experience and sensibilities gained far greater public value, as the compassionate caretakers, educators, and managers, more concerned with the qualitative than the quantitative aspects and amenities of life.

American philanthropy has met challenges, and taken advantage of opportunities, that neither government nor business usually address. The other sectors certainly affect our quality of life, but philanthropy focuses on it. If we look around us, and thoroughly survey the multitude of specific "private initiatives for public good, focusing on quality of life," we may begin to appreciate what a stake we all have in the vitality of personal and institutional philanthropy, including our own, and collectively that of our philanthropic sector.

At the same time, it is probably true that American philanthropy has not since that first great flowering, achieved the self-conscious power and productivity, nobility and grandeur in our culture, that it manifested in the American Revolution. That is still our shining example of what a "philanthropic culture" can be, and how—manifested in individual lives—it can produce superior human beings like Benjamin Franklin and so many of our other Founders in their greatest work. It also suggests that the United States of America was, at its birth, intended to be a philanthropic nation in the world. It even suggests what great good American philanthropy might accomplish in today's world—and let that be a lesson for us all.

III. Philanthropy Yesterday and Today: Paradigm-Formation and -Shift

A. Introduction and Overview

Chapter I explored the original meaning of "philanthropy," from its first recorded use in the 5th century BCE *Prometheus Bound*, through its associations with Greek and Roman philosophy, education and culture, up to early Christianity. From this etymology and history we defined a "Classical, humanistic" view of philanthropy in modern terms, as potentially useful to philanthropy today.

Chapter II showed that the Classical view has in fact already influenced modern history—how it emerged from its medieval hibernation into a strong position in early-modern English, hence American Colonial, thought and practice; how it informed the Enlightenment, especially in Scotland and the Colonies; how it was strengthened at the practical level by necessity in Colonial life to become habitual routine in "voluntary associations"; and how all that—Classical philanthropy, in action—played a leading role and is an essential key to understanding the American Revolution and the founding of our nation.

Chapter III takes the opposite tack—to show how the **lack** of the Classical or any other substantive understanding and view of philanthropy has also "mattered." In the late 20th-century, the American philanthropic sector grew and professionalized more than ever before, so that it became paradigmatic—an orderly system. For all its institutional, technical, and procedural strengths, and genuine great benefactions, however, that paradigm did not achieve anything approaching the cultural influence or historic accomplishments of the earlier period. This is obviously not, and not intended as, a devastating criticism, but it is worth noting, and we shall explain how and why it was so.

New developments in the environment of the sector and moving into it have now instigated a paradigm-shift, affecting both the sector and its relations with the general public. The main exogenous causes of the paradigm-shift in philanthropy are: the revolution in information technology, the globalization of the American economy, and the attendant changing demographics of wealth. Interestingly, the word "philanthropy" itself has reappeared in common usage, so that a clear and authentic definition should be helpful in connecting the word, idea, and cultural phenomenon to our broader culture.

This paradigm-shift analysis was originally proposed in two articles in *Foundation News*, in 2000; since then, events and developments have confirmed the diagnosis, and clarified the prognosis about an unfolding new paradigm. This chapter is not, however, a systematically researched history, but rather an interpretive essay based on direct observations over the past twenty-five years' of practical experience at the grassroots of the sector.

Paradigm-shifts are complex, dramatic, and exciting historical phenomena. They have real winners and losers, for whom the stakes are high. The story is enlarged by the literary and historic contexts proposed in Chapters I and II, which in effect see the entire drama on a much larger stage. In that context, this chapter reveals the coherent argument being developed in this wide-ranging small book—aimed squarely at the subject of Chapter IV: the future of American philanthropy. That is a subject in which we are all stakeholders.

I emphasize that this is a positive interpretation, constructively intended. While it does identify certain flaws or dysfunctions in what we call the Old Paradigm, it is important to know that all paradigms have flaws, and that identifying them helps their development. In this case also we see them as rooms for improvement in the venerable mansion of philanthropy. Those renovations are what the shift to a New Paradigm, outlined in Chapter IV, is now accomplishing.

B. Background: A Note on the Importance of Secularity

One of the central flaws of the Old Paradigm, seen from the perspective and in the context of Chapters I and II, is less a flaw of the emerging Paradigm itself than of the culture around it, which it necessarily reflected.

Chapters I and II dealt with the ancient Classical world and the early-modern period in Western thought, when it was assumed that the world is a coherent whole—a universe—to be dealt with as such in thought (religion and philosophy, and a university of learning in which scholarship and science are unified) and practice.

Chapter III is about the late 20th century, which is an entirely different cultural *milieu*—a secular culture, which is intrinsically fragmented. Secular culture, for various historical reasons, generally avoids—in fact it evolved in the modern era purposefully to avoid—the whole question of the unity and coherence of reality. It does so by thinking about and dealing with the world as if it were divided into separate parts—a "multiverse," as Henry Adams first (late 19th century) aptly described it, studied by "multiversity" scholarship (as Clark Kerr and James Perkins pointed out in the 1960s).

The essence of secularity is fragmentation of life and thought—that is what opposes it to religion and philosophies like Stoicism, which are predicated on the assumption that the world is a coherent whole and that life should be lived in accordance or in harmony with how that ultimate coherence is defined. The Classical view of philanthropy was formulated within a universalist world-view, which was still powerful in the late 18th century (though disintegration was already well under way).

The point of this aside is that when we cite as a weakness of the Old Paradigm that it lacked the profound philosophical framework of Classical philanthropy, this is only to say that it, like the culture around it, was (is) secular, and to that extent and in that way, perforce, superficial. The Old Paradigm in philanthropy was a result, rather than a cause, of modern American secularity.

C. Background—Paradigm-Shifts and Philanthropy

The words "paradigm" and "paradigm-shift" are so commonly used, in so many ways, that we had better define what we mean by them here.

Historians divide history into distinctive "periods," in which a culture, for example, manifests identifiable characteristics—e.g., the "Renaissance" or the "Reformation" in European history, or the "Colonial" or "Federal" periods in American history.

Thomas Kuhn, in *The Structure of Scientific Revolutions* (1962), introduced a distinction between two kinds of periods in the history of sciences. Most of the time, any science has "normal" periods, when all scientists in a field work in complementary ways, following a shared set of conventions—i.e., generally agreed-upon basic assumptions, methods, instruments, and interests. Those conventions, taken together, Kuhn said, constitute a "paradigm" or governing model, for the science in question.

Occasionally however, in the history of any science, there are "revolutionary" periods, in which a traditional paradigm is fundamentally challenged or called into question, often by influences from outside the paradigm— e.g., new technology, or new discoveries—that challenge the paradigm fundamentally, forcing a search for a new paradigm. Periods of scientific revolution are characterized by what Kuhn called "paradigm-shift," when a science is "between paradigms"—moving out of an old outmoded one and toward an as-yet undefined new one.

Kuhn's terminology is especially suitable for the history of science, because sciences are systematic. Historians of non-scientific fields, however, have found these terms useful in varying degrees, as their subjects are more or less rigorously organized, like the sciences. In Chapter II for example we referred to R.R. Palmer's definition of political revolutions as "unconstitutional changes in the constitution of a polity," which amounts to paradigm-shifts in politics.

American philanthropy is obviously far less organized than the natural sciences, and of course has nothing like a written political constitution or body of laws. Neither amateur nor professional philanthropists see themselves as participating in any particular period, nor their practices ordered by any particular paradigm or governing model. Nonetheless, Kuhn's terminology illuminates where we are now in the history of modern philanthropy.

Everyone in philanthropy today agrees that many important changes are occurring in our field; the question for us here is whether these are simply evolutionary (normal change) or revolutionary—**fundamental, irreversible, structural and strategic changes**, imposed from outside the realms of normal practice. If they are the latter, we are in a period of paradigm-shift— out of a relatively settled period with its own distinctive governing pattern, into a less settled period but moving perceptibly toward some new, as yet undefined, governing pattern, model, system, or paradigm.

This is an extraordinarily significant issue. If philanthropy is being transformed or revolutionized, it matters to everyone involved—though it is characteristic of paradigm-shifts that those most deeply engaged in the Old Paradigm are generally the last to recognize and adapt to what is happening. The direction of our field as it moves into the future will affect whatever one does, whether that is likely to succeed, and what will be its results.

Persons considering entering philanthropy in any capacity, and especially young people, should be planning and preparing for the future, not the past or even the present. Paradigm-shifts create and empower new possibilities, so it helps to be alert to what those might be and how to take practical advantage of them—to identify problems that are being resolved, and align with the solutions—to identify probable winners and losers, and join the winners.

Moreover, in periods of paradigm-shift, structures are unusually fluid and flexible. It is much easier to effect changes in changing times. Change is constant and inevitable, but if we can identify the key fundamental structural and strategic changes occurring at a given moment in history, we can work to facilitate and expedite them, to "go with the flow" so that it is less disruptive to our own lives and those of others, and so we shall come out ahead of where we would have been otherwise.

D. The Emergence of the 20th-Century Paradigm

The last half of the twentieth century was a coherent and distinctive period in the history of American philanthropy, marked by field-transforming **growth** and **professionalization**—each nourishing the other, informed by characteristic technology and institutions of the period, producing distinctive results.

1. Growth
First we must note that descriptions of the philanthropic sector have been technically inadequate, because the main data on which everyone relies was conceived, articulated, and developed by the IRS, for other purposes, and because our basic vocabulary—even what 'philanthropy' means—has been inconsistent and imprecise. Thus for example there is no agreement on what fields there are in philanthropy, nor on the numbers of charities within them. There is light at the end of this tunnel, because computerization has rapidly multiplied data, but we aren't there yet. We are increasingly enabled, and will eventually be compelled, to define and clarify everything about philanthropy.

The 1975 *Bicentennial...Historical Statistics of the United States* barely mentioned what it clumsily called (which is notable in itself) "Nonprofit membership organizations" (this would include such things as yacht clubs, but never mind). The report focused on their economic significance (because that is all that could be statisticized)—e.g., their accelerating growth in share of income, personnel, and earnings (i.e., **not** their number, even) for the forty years since the 1929 census and up to 1970. In that 40-year period, those institutions' **income** doubled in the 18 years from 1929-1947, and then redoubled more rapidly, about every 8-10 years up to 1975; doublings of **payrolls** occurred about every 20 years, and of average **earnings** from 1929-'59 (30 years), and again before 1975 (16 years).

Everyone agrees that since 1970 growth has continued to accelerate, though reports and estimates vary. Lester Salamon, in **America's Nonprofit Sector** (1999, 2nd Edition) reported that in the period 1970-1996, the sector's **employees** multiplied from 1.4 to 10.9 million (nearly 8x), while its total **income** rocketed from $8.4 billion to $670.3 billion (nearly 80x!). Peter Dobkin Hall has reported that in the 8 years 1982-90 the number of institutions increased by 24%. Independent Sector has reported that in the next decade (1989-1999), expenditures more than quadrupled (from $189 billion to $785 billion); and at about the same time (1987-1997) the number of charities, foundations and religious organizations increased by 31%, and the workforce by 27% (from 8.6 million to 10.9 million, 1988-1998). The *Wall Street Journal* reported in 2006 that "Already, over the past 10 years, there's been an 88% increase in the number of foundations ...[and] a 67% growth in the overall number of U.S. nonprofits." From 1995 to 2005, private foundations increased 49%, to 77,000; 67% of the new ones had assets below $1 million, 27% more were less than $10 million, so only 6% had assets above $10 million. An important cause was favorable tax incentives, indicated as rules in the 80's and made law into 1998. In short, everybody agrees on rapid accelerating growth, but not on the details, because the experts are evidently not counting the same things.

2. Professionalization: The Sector Organizes Along Occupational Lines

As the rapid and accelerating growth occurred, the various occupations in philanthropy were separately organizing for professional development and certification. Grantmakers formed the Council on Foundations, the Foundation Center, Regional Associations of Grantmakers (RAGs), and associations of "Small," "Family," "Community," and corporate, foundations. Fundraisers formed the National Society of Fund Raising Executives (NSFRE—now AFP, the Association of Fundraising Professionals), the American Association of Fund-Raising Counsel (AAFRC—consultants, as distinct from staff), and more specialized groups of women, healthcare, planned giving, capital campaign, etc., fundraisers. Executive Directors formed various state and regional "Non-Profit Associations"; Independent Sector (IS) sought to combine all three constituencies. The *Chronicle of Philanthropy* was founded as the weekly newspaper of the entire field, to serve all the above and especially to organize their job markets. Graduate programs in universities were created to train future "non-profit" executives in all these capacities.

Organizing philanthropy along occupational lines, and professionalizing the occupations through technical training and certification, was a deliberate strategy of the major national foundations. For example, the Ford Foundation's "Governance and Civil Society" Program was created to play a leading role in this movement, helping to create the Council on Foundations, The Foundation Center, Independent Sector, the National Council on Nonprofit Associations, and the Forum of Regional Associations of Grantmakers. In the 1980s Ford also supported new graduate-level academic programs training professional philanthropists (e.g., at Indiana, Yale, the City University of New York, Duke and Johns Hopkins), and new philanthropic research entities: the Aspen Institute Nonprofit Sector Research Fund, the Association for Research on Nonprofit and Voluntary Action (ARNOVA), the International Society for Third Sector Research, *et al.* Ford also encouraged the proliferation of special-interest grantmaker groups within the Council on Foundations, around issues and ethnicities. Within each network, communications and connections intensified, which promoted shared technical terminology, values, agendas, and strategies characteristic of professional cohorts. Donors generally were not organized, though federated giving programs (e.g., United Way, Community Chests, etc.) were created, often led by corporations as part of their civic responsibilities, and managed by professional staffs.

3. Growth and Professionalization in a Positive Feedback Loop Create a Paradigm

Growth and professionalization fed each other, to produce in the last half of the 20th century a system that acquired paradigmatic influence.

Technology is always a defining influence in paradigms. The technology for philanthropy in the late twentieth century consisted primarily of the telephone, the typewriter, the printing press, printed materials, and the print and broadcast media—generally very expensive for charities to use, with high dependence on professional staff. As the period progressed, the development of mainframe computerized databases in government and the largest charities, and the industrialization of fundraising in mass-produced direct-mail, telemarketing, and nationally televised "telethons," evolved into increasingly large-scale systems.

The numbers of new charities (by which we mean charitable, philanthropic, corporations, as distinct from "non-profits") were exploding, in creative responses to newly emerging public issues and opportunities. Charities are created by "private initiatives for public good, focusing on quality of life." In general, their founders are generous, caring, intelligent, energetic, civic-minded individuals—problem-solvers and entrepreneurs. Not all of them are skillful institution-builders, but most are intent on growing their institutions, to survive and flourish. Almost all new charities start small, and they have a life-cycle from infancy through youth, adolescence, maturity, seniority, and ultimately (with few exceptions) demise. As they grow, their budgets increase, their staffs become more professional, they become more institutionalized, their boards become more strategic than tactical, more focused on policies than particular operations, and they acquire professional staffs specializing in institution-building functions, especially fundraising and public relations, which push further program growth.

The ideal model for both charities and foundations in this period was, emulating the commercial sector, the large national corporation. This worked well for a very small number of national and some local or regional institutions, led by universities, hospitals, and health organizations, but in every field, plus a few private and community foundations. Their budgets, personal networks, and financial assets, tended to be large to begin with so that they could readily fuel and achieve further growth and systematic development. Their fundraisers were the first to professionalize, organizing their alumni and their databases for fundraising purposes, perfecting the techniques of annual appeals, capital campaigns, and constant direct-mail solicitations. They passed on these techniques to their colleagues in smaller organizations, through their national professional associations.

Foundations, though they provided only about 10% of the private dollars in philanthropy (corporations only about 5%), especially as their staffs became increasingly professionalized, set the agendas. Their grants were the most cost-effective and quickest way to fund growth. This was the age of glory for the small number of very large national foundations, created by the great private fortunes amassed earlier in the century by titans of capitalism—Rockefeller, Ford, Carnegie, Mellon, Pew, *et al.*

As the numbers of grant-seeking charities multiplied however, foundations informally responded with what seemed to be a series of increasingly narrowly-focused and more highly leveraged grantmaking strategies, at each step intended to reduce competition and increase results, stretching the impacts of their slower-growing endowment yields. Each step was countered successfully, however, by increasingly crafty fundraisers. This dialectic helps to explain the wary and uneasy, though superficially friendly, relations between grantmakers and fundraisers.

In the 1950s **general operating support grants** were relatively common, and most foundations had stables of favored charities that they helped support with regular, reliable, crucial, unrestricted dollars.

Then, as proposals increased, the foundations weaned their favorites from general operating support to **project grants**, seeking specified results for specified costs (the interest in quantification trumpeted today is by no means a new development). At decision-making tables, attractive and compelling project grants designed by professional fundraisers competed favorably, owing to their concreteness and specificity, against requests for general operating support. The fundraisers therefore learned to package their general operations proposals as projects, and proposals kept increasing.

So grantmakers focused on **new projects**, as distinct from customary operations; fine, the fundraisers learned to play that game, too. The next step was **new and innovative** projects, showing that what was intended was not only new for the organization, but an innovative model for others. Still the proposals multiplied, so the next step was a shift to wean charities from foundation support itself, with new, innovative projects **that could become self-supporting** when the start-up funds ran out, often after three years. Subsequently, foundations focused on "**capacity-building**" grants, also intended to free charities from dependence on foundation grants—hiring fundraising, membership and public relations staffs, developing **earned-income** programs, extending networks of personal donors, developing direct-mail programs addressing the general public, etc.

This drift toward increasing specialization of grants, and what appeared to be ever-changing fads and fancies of grantmakers, was increasingly felt by charities as stress. They protested and appealed nostalgically for a return to the salad days of general operating support. These protests failed because the evolution of grantmaking strategies was driven by objective forces, primarily increased competition for less rapidly increasing grant dollars.

The point is that institutional growth and professionalization for the most successful charities was built-into this system and sequence. Thus increasing technical sophistication of fundraising, and the multiplication of grantseeking charities, inclined the entire system toward growth, and favored the largest, most professionalized charities. What all this amounted to was a positive-feedback loop, appropriate to a period of relatively steady national economic growth.

E. Problems Emerge

But paradigms work well only for a time, because the world into which they must fit is always changing around them. Gradually problems appear, especially at the interfaces with their environments, and either structures adapt, and the paradigm's order is maintained and strengthened; or the problems persist as low-level irritants; or they grow and multiply, to the point of challenging or undermining the paradigm itself (often together with other problems). A common pattern is that changes in the environment of the paradigm exacerbate problems within the paradigm itself, until its viability is fundamentally challenged by a combination of external and internal conflicts which it cannot resolve. Such was the case in late-20th-century philanthropy. The philanthropic sector is like an ecosystem, in which adequate supply, and broad circulation and distribution of energy, smooth functioning of interdependent parts, and stable or increasing biodiversity, are signs of health; their opposites are not.

1. Compartmentalization—Lack of Community

Modern philanthropy has customarily been particularistic—individual charities reaching out to individual donors, and vice-versa, through informal personal networks. Among charities, which were increasing in number faster than the increase in philanthropic and government dollars available, the atmosphere was felt to be increasingly competitive, in an economy of scarcity (i.e., of dollars). Competition discouraged collaboration, and foreclosed strategic options, despite the fact that grantmakers explicitly encouraged collaborative proposals (again, to stretch their dollars).

The compartmentalization of philanthropy into separate occupational constituencies also limited strategic options, as the various groups talked mainly to themselves, about themselves and their own technical development. The word "philanthropy" was rarely used. The phrase "philanthropic community" was occasionally used, but more as a rhetorical than a strategic device—something that existed only in principle. Extremely few, if any, institutions or professional person's jobs, focused on philanthropy itself, as a whole—it simply was not an item of significant interest or concern; nobody was thinking, saying, or doing, anything about it as a whole. Grantmakers, in periodic reports on "the state of philanthropy," even used the word to refer solely to themselves!

A possible exception which however proves the rule was the *Chronicle of Philanthropy*, co-founded by the same publisher as the highly profitable *Chronicle of Higher Education*, as a "sister publication" (their phrase). It was created, not to illuminate philanthropy or the sector as a whole for strategic purposes, but mainly to serve its various occupational constituencies and especially job markets profitably, through economies of scale, and to conform with Affirmative Action guidelines requiring broad publicity of job openings. The *Chronicle* is an immensely valuable and authoritative publication, relied upon by nearly everyone in the sector, presenting mountains of information. That said, its strengths reflect the particularism and fragmentation of the sector, of academic scholarship, and of our secular culture, with hardly any attention to philanthropy as a whole, its interface with the public as a whole, its greatest accomplishments as a whole, and its strategic role as a whole in national culture or affairs. Articles tend to focus on individuals and individual institutions, and—unfortunately and misleadingly—scandals, with very little attention to how the pieces fit together, i.e., very little grasp of the whole. Again, this particularist bias has reflected the particularism of the late-twentieth-century paradigm in philanthropy.

Another possible exception to this rule of fragmentation of the constituencies might have been Independent Sector (IS), which was created in the early '80s to represent everyone, to be "the umbrella organization of the sector," a common forum. This perhaps signified that the fragmentation of the putative "philanthropic community" was considered problematic, at least with regard to advocacy with government. After ten years however, it had only 600 institutional members—300 (large) charities, 150 (large) foundations, and 150 (large) corporations.

As IS's name indicates, however, the organization was dominated by the foundations, which are the only institutions in philanthropy that do or can think of themselves, individually and collectively, as "independent"—which they are, owing to their endowments—until, that is, they run up against government. Most charities by far are painfully aware that they are not individually or collectively "independent" of anyone or anything—they depend entirely on foundations, corporations, government, and donors, for their dollars (when IS was founded, small charities were just beginning to develop earned-income as a significant source of funds). The principle motivation for creating IS was to prevent more effectively government regulation, by advocacy and creating a structure that would dramatize the value of the sector's independence from government. To its credit, IS did mount a *pro bono* advertising campaign that I recall as a member, to increase charitable giving from 2% to 5% of income—"Give Five" was the slogan. After a while it petered out without success. IS has also sponsored very helpful statistical surveys of the sector, published in several desk-reference compendia. IS continues as a perpetual hope, but its mission and strategies have been more preventive of governmental excesses, than noticeably strengthening philanthropy as a whole in this crucial growth-period.

Compartmentalization also divided the culture of the sector in disadvantageous ways. **Grantmakers** tended to regard **fundraisers** increasingly as adversaries rather than as colleagues. **Charities** were, and felt, condescended to by grantmakers, who at their few joint meetings made patronizing remarks presuming to set rules of decorum for the charities—e.g., that it would be inappropriate to "conduct business," meaning to cultivate or solicit grants. **Donors** operated individually, without benefit of organization or systems of outreach from the sector to the donating public as a whole. **Journalists** and the **media** were largely ignorant of philanthropy, because the professionals did not teach it. The **public's** knowledge was restricted to their own personal experiences with individual charities. **Scholarship** in the field was in its infancy, coming at philanthropy from, and often publishing for, the various (fragmented) social sciences rather than for a readership spanning all philanthropy.

The cumulative result of compartmentalization was that these constituencies did not feel that they were all on the same team, that they were equal shareholders in a larger single community of philanthropy. They were not formally aware of any shared responsibilities for and to the concept, the values, or the sector as a whole.

2. Dysfunctional Economy

Above all, these various compartmentalized constituencies formally neglected, where they did not ignore altogether, individual donors as a constituency—which is remarkable because the ignored group provided not just most, but 85%, of the private dollars in the sector, through annual giving and charitable bequests.

The accelerating increase in numbers of charities meant that an increasing portion of the total were small. Because their budgets were small, they could not afford professional non-program institutional development staff—e.g., in fundraising and public relations. Nor could they afford broad public visibility using print media. As a result, over 90% of charities were invisible to the general public, who provided 85% of the private dollars in the sector. That is a dysfunctional economy of charitable giving.

To make matters worse from the point of view of distribution of energy and resources, corporate and private foundations were allocating almost all their 15% of the private dollars to the very small number of already-wealthiest charities whose fundraisers were the most technically skilled professionals. One study reported that 80% of grant dollars were flowing to the top 5% of charities—those with budgets above $5 million—and that the lowest-budget 80% of charities were receiving only 5% of grant dollars. This meant that the top 5% of charities were capturing 12% of the 15% of corporate and foundation grantmaking dollars, leaving everyone else to compete against each other for the remaining 3%. That is also a dysfunctional economy within grantmaking.

3. Dysfunctional Economies Undermine Culture

This goes a long way toward explaining why, as one study reported, only one in twelve grant proposals nationwide, all fields, were funded; 11 of the 12 were declined. Charities below the top 5% were living in a culture of rejection by grantmakers, and ignorance by donors, underpaid and overworked, unappreciated by the media and the public—for their "private initiatives for public good, focusing on quality of life," after all. Surveys show that "quality of life" is the No. 1 issue of concern to everyone, and yet generally speaking, very few people realize how much quality of life in our society depends—not just on the very few largest, wealthiest, highly visible, charities—but on the philanthropic sector as a whole, of which almost no one knows anything.

Some of the larger charities also generated cultural problems by turning to broad public fundraising with industrial methods: direct-mail and telemarketing. These seemed at first to be potent, but turned out to be problematic because the public did not like what they regarded as unsolicited "junk" mail or "junk" telephone calls. As a result, the **rates** of return were very small—1-3% responses. In huge volume that raised considerable funds, but in the process alienated 97-99% of those solicited, which was a very broad segment of the public. Moreover, the donors generating the large numbers of small gifts elicited by these obnoxious methods enjoyed very little "donor-satisfaction." Study after study has found that only about 30% of the total dollars raised by those industrial methods found their way to programs, as against fundraising costs and overhead, so that each donor's small contribution was a drop in the ocean floating the tip of the iceberg. This was not an economic system that could produce a healthy long-term financial future, and it was certainly not a system that defined, much less promoted, a robust culture of philanthropy in society as a whole.

4. Culture—Knowledge, Vocabulary, Conceptualization, Rhetoric

This matter of culture is crucial. The vocabulary, rhetoric and conceptualization of philanthropy in this age of flourishing growth and professionalization was not informed by anything approaching the Classical view of philanthropy, much less any understanding of philanthropy's role in creating and establishing this nation. Intellectual energy focused on techniques and procedures, rather than content, of communications, enabled by a kind of "logapathy"—not caring what words mean—a rarified zone into which words (often without any appropriate intellectual content) immigrated or were imported from outside philanthropy (mainly the IRS and the social sciences). Once here, they evolved uncritically, into technical jargon with a remarkably negative tone, lacking potency, donor-friendliness, and inspiration. No one noticed, because it was no institution's or person's job to pay attention to such things, even among the leadership of the sector. This is evidence of obliviousness to donors.

As a result, the late 20th-century paradigm in philanthropy was culturally characterized by what amounted to self-absorption, and (as compared with the Classical tradition) superficiality. It tended to focus exclusively on itself and on procedural issues, inconsiderate of substantive issues and its environment. To be fair, this "exclusive specialization" happens to be the dominant pattern throughout our secular culture, promoted in the structures and strategies of our academic and educational systems. Nor can one say these were "failures," because their opposites—concern for the environment of philanthropy, and for substance as distinct from procedures— were not even tried. The philanthropic profession, which was flourishing in so many ways, did not try to create a "philanthropic culture" within its own sector, much less in America as a purportedly philanthropic nation. This is what happens when the word "philanthropy" is neglected.

Two salient examples are terms borrowed from the IRS: "non-profit" and "tax-exempt." Note that both are negative. What the IRS does is tax, and what it taxes are profits; translated into English, what those terms mean to the IRS is "doesn't matter"—a negative locution, serving a positive function **within the IRS**: to sort them out from what does matter. From the IRS's perspective what matters about non-profits and exempt entities is what they are not and do not. But the minute these words, and the attitudes behind them, wander, drift, or are appropriated outside the IRS, they become dysfunctional. Why the professionalizing philanthropic community so carelessly adopted these impertinences, without bothering to consider their value to what we are and do, especially in our life-blood activity of fundraising, is beyond me.

The profundity of the error is remarkable. Since the dawn of human history (never mind civilization) language has been customarily and progressively used to name things for what they are and do, not for what they aren't and don't. The positive approach is what makes language a tool. It would be meaningless and, frankly, stupid, to call a cat a "non-dog," and if this sort of thing were commonplace, we'd still be living in darkness and caves—the Promethean fire would have flickered out, and Zeus would have terminated the human experiment.

The only excuse ever offered for these ludicrous technical terms is their conventionality—which is, let's face it, logapathetic. There is absolutely no need for them in philanthropy—ordinary English can handle what we are and do. The word "charities" covers all charitable corporations; the word "philanthropy" covers the sector precisely and nicely; alternatives like "the benefit sector" have been proposed to distinguish it from "the profit sector." Moreover, it is inconsiderate to pretend that the negative "non-profit" signifies anything desirable to donors, whose money comes from "profits," and who believe that being profitable is evidence of skill and intelligence.

So for fundraising, empty terminology at the heart of our enterprise is ridiculously wasted opportunity, and demonstrably counterproductive. In fact, the term "non-profit" as applied to the philanthropic sector is also factually quite inaccurate and misleading (see Appendix One).

These were not isolated *faux pas*—there were others. Within fundraising, philanthropy and charitable giving were customarily referred to as "giving away," "giving back," through "non-profits," "non-governmental" or "tax-exempt" organizations" in the "third" (out of three) sector, for the "disadvantaged," the "have-nots," the "at-risk" people. The negative drift of these expressions is, however inadvertently so, clearly uninspired and uninspiring.

And how are people persuaded to support something described vacuously and negatively? By reference to moral obligation of course—"ought" and "should." The suggestion is that even though they may not enjoy or be inspired by it, people are morally obliged to give, that they **owe** part of what they have earned to others. The problems here are that the sense of obligation detracts or distracts from the pleasures, happiness, and personal rewards of giving, and is never far from guilt-tripping the rich, many of whom resent and are oppressed by it, psychologically and morally.

E. Bottom Lines

One proof of this pudding is the charitable giving it produced. Let us first acknowledge what everyone knows, that Americans are the most philanthropic nation on Earth. For years—decades—the annual *Giving USA* reports have estimated that giving has been increasing. But the same numbers from a different angle, which to their credit AAFRC has also reported, show that charitable giving in the last half-century remained flat, at only about 2% of Gross Domestic Product and less than that for Adjusted Gross Income. According to *Historical Statistics of the United States*, philanthropy compared with the GDP actually declined from 1960 onward. At the close of the century only one in four taxpayers itemized charitable deductions (which account for 80% of private dollars in philanthropy), and fewer than one in five **taxable** estates included any charitable bequests at all.

In other words, while the rest of philanthropy was dramatically expanding and professionalizing, charitable giving under the Old Paradigm was sluggish, in scope and spirit—a marginal interest of Americans.

Moreover, what attracted almost all this giving was, perforce, the only part of philanthropy that was visible to the general public: the tip-of-the-iceberg. But this was not where the dynamic growth and creativity occurred, in the last half of the twentieth century. The most compelling and interesting developments in that period in American philanthropy were subliminal—manifested in the huge majority—over 90%—of charities, who were invisible and unknown to the public. The media neither knew nor (perforce) cared about philanthropy except in connection with scandals, social events, or occasional human-interest stories. The media's customary focus on money, power, and conflict, excluded almost all charities, which were too small to be interesting from that perspective, and in any case about which the media, and thus the public, had no way of knowing. Public knowledge and interest was almost entirely restricted to the largest, most visible, charities, whose activities were stable, predictable, and slow—notably like the charitable giving they attracted.

In short, the Old Paradigm emerged with a systemic—strategic and structural—flaw, which in effect stunted its growth and, consequently, cultural influence. Its most dynamic and creative aspects were invisible to the providers of 85% of its private dollars, which is to say its life's blood. The large, creative, majority of charities was living on the very small percentage of giving, grantmaking, and volunteering that these charities could attract by themselves, working person-to-person in their small networks. The requisite donor education was not being done. Broad public ignorance of philanthropy was not the students' fault—it was that of the professionals who might have been the faculty, were they not almost totally distracted by administrative details.

But as a strategically significant fact this was of course unnoticed—a sort of "dog didn't bark" phenomenon. It is difficult to prove negatives in history—what doesn't happen when certain causes are absent—because there is a corresponding absence of evidence on which to base any positive assertions. What we have suggested here is that in a period when the philanthropic sector was by **almost** all measures flourishing, the only parts that were not, were exceptions for the same reason. That is as close as we can get to a positive assertion, based on evidence.

Similarly, it is true that the events and developments described in this third Chapter, happened without the benefits of what has been shown in Chapters I and II to be advantageous. We know what a "philanthropic culture" looks like in America because we (now) have a precedent with which to compare and contrast the dynamic Old Paradigm and its lack of broad cultural influence. The Old Paradigm's focus on procedural, rather than substantive, issues—on professionalization and growth without much formal attention to the word "philanthropy" or its meaning—foreclosed the possibility of broad or deep cultural influence, which in turn stunted the growth of charitable giving as well. Here again, the lack of substantive and extensive donor education was critical—another case of the dog not barking. Donors were giving according to what they knew and understood about philanthropy, which was not much—again, the faculty's, not the students', fault.

Here, then, is a brief and schematic summary of the emergent paradigm of philanthropy in the last half of the twentieth century:

Old Paradigm—20th Century

Technology: Printing; post-office mail; telephone.

Economy: Traditional diversified 20th-century American—steady growth, generally stable, corporate economy.

Institutions: Private foundations lead;
Community foundations multiply;
Large charities dominate fundraising
by direct mail and telemarketing.

Professional associations established for grantmakers, fundraisers, and charities;

The philanthropic community
divides into occupational constituencies.

National Taxonomy of Exempt Entities
created for research (i.e., not donors).

People: Professionalization makes philanthropy
highly technical.

Practices: Industrialized fundraising—telemarketing,
direct mail, increasingly competitive grantmaking.

Rhetoric: Moral obligation. "Giving away," "Giving Back,"
through "non-profits" or "tax-exempt entities" in
the "third" "sector" to the "needy," the
"disadvantaged."

Results: <2% Gross Domestic Product and Adjusted Gross Income; only 25% Itemizers of Charitable Deductions; <20% taxable estates make charitable bequests; 5% largest charities get 80% grant dollars, 80% smallest charities get 5% grant dollars.

F. The Shift Begins

Paradigm-shifts are most often precipitated by powerful, influential changes coming at them from their environment, which create problems at the borders, weaken the ability of the paradigm to order its realm, and which empower alternatives. In this case the pertinent environmental changes were the revolution in information technology—computers and the Internet—and the globalization of the American economy, which together transformed the demographics of wealth in America in ways that produced dissatisfaction with conventions in philanthropy, and non-conventional alternative approaches.

The first impacts of computerization on philanthropy were not disruptive at all—quite the opposite. They accelerated even more the growth and professionalization especially of the large charities, which could easily afford to take full advantage of the new capabilities. As the costs of computers declined and their power increased, the benefits trickled down to ever-smaller charities, for whom the decisions loomed large of when and how to make their increasingly inevitable transitions from typewriters to word processors to desktop computers. With each progressive step the productivity of small staffs multiplied. Grant-makers were flooded with proposals to computerize operations, and they responded with varying degrees of hospitality and enthusiasm. But the rising tide of computerization in philanthropy lifted all boats. With more, better, and better-managed, data, all philanthropy was being strengthened and refined, though the full benefits were not immediately apparent and will probably take another decade from now to realize.

Similarly, the globalization of the economy in its early stages simply increased wealth, which is always good for philanthropy. From 1997 to 2000 nationwide, Average Adjusted Gross Income increased 39%, while Average Itemized Charitable Deductions (about 80% of total charitable giving) increased 62%—a heartening sign that the new wealth-creators were philanthropic.

1. Communications Open and Increase

As computerization and globalization continued to nourish each other, certain new developments began not only to increase, but to change, philanthropy. The advent of the Internet was a fundamentally transforming influence, because it quickly liberated the more than 90% of all charities with budgets below $2 million, from their confinements by prohibitively expensive print media. Suddenly even the smallest charities could afford to become universally visible and accessible by creating websites in cyberspace, and to communicate more freely and broadly at very low cost. (Getting people to visit their websites was still a problem, but potential solutions were at least not prohibitively expensive.) E-mail radically accelerated, and reduced costs of, communications with members, colleagues and patrons. Flex-time, home offices, and later cell-phones, reduced administrative costs and multiplied productivity. The relative advantages of institutional bigness were reduced and in some cases eliminated; new small charities could more easily be created and survive, rendering the sector as a whole more creative, more responsive to new problems. The world of philanthropy was being flattened, and "private initiatives for public good, focusing on quality of life" were energized as personal and civic options. The body could breath more easily, and circulation improved.

2. New and Emerging Donors

In the 1990s the innovative, high-tech and globalizing economy soared, rapidly creating huge new wealth, especially for younger entrepreneurs who were more interested in and adept with the new technology. The numbers of millionaires, decamillionaires, centimillionaires, and even billionaires, multiplied rapidly, and an extraordinarily large portion of them were relatively young adults. As their "surplus wealth" by any definition accumulated, many turned restlessly to philanthropy as a next step in their careers, to gain a larger sense of the meanings of their hyper-productive lives. This was a substantive, not merely procedural, development for philanthropy.

There was another growth surge in new private foundations; in Massachusetts for example, by 2004 there were 2,642 private foundations, of which 40%—over 1,000— were less than 10 years old. Donor-advised funds—originally developed by community foundations and then commercialized by commercial financial services, multiplied rapidly as facilitators of charitable giving. The so-called "new and emerging donors" (NEDs) attracted intense interest from fundraisers, philanthropic advisors, researchers, and (naturally) the media. The word "philanthropy" was reviving.

But the NEDs turned out to be generally critical of conventional philanthropy. Believing that their own extraordinary great fortunes came from aggressively innovative thinking-outside-the-box, many of them believed they could get similarly spectacular results in making the world a better place, by re-thinking philanthropy as well. They didn't "buy" the rhetoric of "giving back" (they did not believe their wealth was "given" to them), nor of "giving away" (what they had worked so hard, so rapidly and recently, to gain), and they were in no mood for the moralistic, guilt-tripping, rhetoric of their duty or obligation to give, that had persuaded their elderly predecessors.

Working from what they knew best, the NEDs presumed that charities should be run more like entrepreneurial businesses, that grantseeking should be just like raising venture capital, with close attention to business plans and "the numbers"—quantified measurements and predictions of productivity, and close accountability to quantitative benchmarks of success. They readily concluded that the philanthropic sector was technically backward, and needed to tighten-up its business skills and competitive spirit. They preferred to make small numbers of large, rather than large numbers of small, "investments," which made them a highly attractive and prominent target for fundraisers. They were investing in dramatic growth, in bringing charities "to scale," and when they made growth investments, just as in the venture capital world, they expected to participate in decisions about how their money was to be spent, and to monitor closely its cost-effectiveness. Generally they believed that their highly entrepreneurial and technically sophisticated skill-sets, which they believed were responsible for their unprecedented business successes, were directly and advantageously transferable to philanthropy. They saw themselves as change-agents, actively and explicitly opposed to what we have here called the "Old Paradigm."

3. Donor Education and Promoting Philanthropy Emerge as New Fields

The sheer heft of the wealth they were bringing to the table—larger donations than most, and sometimes all, foundation grants—and the material rewards of playing things their way, made them a very conspicuous and influential force for change. Since they were new to philanthropy, a "donor education" movement arose to greet them and to try to facilitate their entry. At the retail level was a rapidly increasing number of entrepreneurial "philanthropic advisors" such as The Philanthropic Initiative in Boston (est. 1987); various self-help systems like Seattle's Social Venture Partners (1997), which originated among the "Microsoft millionaires" and spread to other "new economy" centers nationwide; and "giving circles"—e.g., Boston's Hestia Fund (est. 2000) for women philanthropists. At the wholesale level, addressing an entire philanthropic "market" (Massachusetts), was the *Catalogue for Philanthropy* (est. 1997), which resonated nationwide and abroad.

"Promoting philanthropy" and charitable giving also emerged in the late '90s as a new professional sub-field. A few state-level projects had already emerged (e.g., Massachusetts, Connecticut), and at the national level Michael Seltzer at the Ford Foundation organized "New Ventures"—a collaboration of large foundations, to commit $10 million in challenge grants to evoke local and regional projects nationwide, promoting philanthropy and charitable giving. To encourage the involvement of the traditional grantmakers establishments, coordinating the project was intentionally assigned to the national Forum of Regional Associations of Grantmakers (RAGs) in Washington D.C., and local projects were encouraged to be coordinated by local RAGs, who were charged with helping to raise local matching funds. It turned out to be difficult to raise grantmakers' support for projects promoting philanthropy through education of the "new and emerging donors"; the projects received less support than they needed, and rarely outlasted their initial three years under national start-up funding.

4. Commercial Innovation—Sectoral Boundaries Blur
Another clear sign of inflexibility and inhospitality at the borders of traditional philanthropy was that the IRS's distinction between "profit" and "non-profit" was proving to be a false dichotomy in philanthropy. "Private initiatives for public good, focusing on quality of life" could easily be either for-profit or not—in fact, the boundary between the categories was not a sharp line, but a phased spectrum, and had no relevance to whether philanthropic benefaction occurred. Many found it quite possible to "do well by doing good."

A whole new range of philanthropy-related businesses sprang up in the '90s. The financial services industry saw an opportunity with the NEDs and responded creatively; private banks developed donor education programs as value-added services; we have already alluded to the donor-advised "charitable gift funds" created by money managers and resisted by some community foundations.

There are many examples of for-profit businesses being created or used to support charities—one of the best known early examples is Paul Newman's prepared-food business, "Newman's Own," the profits of which support his philanthropy. Google, when it went public, was explicitly committed to philanthropy as a sideline; it later created a $2 billion corporate foundation to fund both for-profit and not-for-profit beneficial initiatives. Buzz Schmidt created GuideStar to assist donors by providing IRS Form 990 returns of charities; he was urged to make it for-profit, but to his credit steadfastly refused; it found a middle way, staying philanthropic but charging considerable fees for services. That model was replicated many times, with services purporting to help donors evaluate charities or facilitate e-giving. Doug Mellinger created FoundationSource, to do for private foundations what the Charitable Gift Funds had done for donor-advised funds. The NEDs were not only comfortable with the hybridization occurring at the interfaces between philanthropy and commerce, but were naturally interested in its possibilities for profit.

5. Inflexibility of the Old Paradigm to Change
But this strategy had quite mixed results. Here again there were signs that the Old Paradigm was coming apart at the seams. Foundations were understandably (though shortsightedly) reluctant to support projects aimed at the highly affluent NEDs. The new boutique industry of retail donor-educators had difficulty supporting themselves on fees for services, because donors were reluctant to pay for consultants in philanthropy, and they understandably (though mistakenly) resisted the notion that they needed "education" (their experiences with formal education had often not been inspiring, and had even been felt to impede their technological take-offs— they were impatient to get on with it).

Seltzer had difficulties securing dollar commitments from the largest foundations, which were echoed at regional and local levels as well. In effect, traditional foundations, which had set the agenda for philanthropy under the Old Paradigm, were choosing not to participate in what was at the turn of the 21st century the most significant development in philanthropy— a telling indicator of paradigm-shift. It seemed to many observers, after repeated examples of foundation reticence, that the older foundations did not consider themselves to be stakeholders in the health and vitality of the philanthropic sector as a whole, as it was evolving, but were focused rigidly and exclusively on their own narrower traditional program agendas. Given that complacency, they had neither need nor desire to move with the new developments in philanthropy. In this case their strength—which is their independence, based on their independent endowments—was a weakness for the Old Paradigm of philanthropy in rapidly, fundamentally, changing times.

Another test of the Old Paradigm's health and vitality was its hospitality to the NEDs. Were these new players graciously welcomed and made to feel at home, perhaps assisted in becoming acquainted with their new neighborhood, or not? Here the evidence is mixed to be sure, but again, on the whole, the Old Paradigm was further weakened by the encounter. Some community foundations like Silicon Valley welcomed the new donors and flourished as a result. Many of the new wealth-creators created their own private, often family, foundations, and some RAGs successfully welcomed them, but many not only did not, but even alienated the new young foundations with inhospitable new-membership fee structures and inadequate services. Fundraisers, having unwisely positioned themselves solely as the sales force for their particular and mostly large charities, failed to take this opportunity to serve also as the faculty for philanthropy as a whole; they treated the new donor-investors as hot donor-prospects for their individual charities, with mixed results. Short-term success in those transactions often encouraged NEDs to look in other directions for their long-term futures in philanthropy as a whole.

G. Conclusion

The situation at the turn of the 20th–21st centuries, then, was that the dominant paradigm was being challenged around its edges by new developments at its borders and in its environment—in technology, in the economy, in the demographics of wealth, in the rejection of traditional conventions by new and emerging donors, and in various unconventional innovations in philanthropy itself. Responses from within the Paradigm were generally not promising for its future—tending to be insensitive, often more negative than positive, suggesting a hardening of its arteries. When an existing Paradigm shows inability constructively to accommodate, facilitate, enable or empower new factors that promise to endure, it signals the end of that era. The stage was set for paradigm-shift, and philanthropy was opening to a new future.

IV. The Future of Philanthropy

A. Paradigm-Shifts in General

Again we ask, so what? What difference does the paradigm-shift analysis make? Does it clarify either the present or the future, in empowering ways, with practical value? This chapter will answer these questions affirmatively.

It is of course impossible to predict the outcomes of paradigm-shifts in detail, because the changes occurring are transformations—thorough, structural, strategic, and fundamental. Not only the rules of the game, but even the games themselves, can change. Therefore any analysis of paradigm-shift, and certainly this one, must be tentative, hypothetical, extraordinarily open-minded, and respectful of complexity.

On the other hand, because paradigm-shifts are **irreversible** changes in **fundamental** structures and strategies, some of the basic outlines of the future paradigm, or aspects of the old paradigm that will probably disappear, may be tentatively identified along the way. Granted that particular **agents** in the process, in even basic outlines—for example in this case the communications revolution—may themselves be often dramatically changing, so that their own outcomes are unpredictable, it may nonetheless be possible to identify the directions of their trends, to foresee their next steps (which are in the case of communications technology already being designed), and to confirm them as fundamental preconditions or premises of any new paradigm.

Besides identifying the most powerful change-agents, a key question is, to what might these various salient elements be **mutually** conducive? **Causation in history is the coincidence of mutually conducive conditions.** As those accumulate in and around a given possibility, the range of their **mutual** possibilities narrows, to ever-higher probabilities and ultimately a certainty when the outcome occurs (this also means that if you want to cause something to happen, pile-up and connect the conducives). The shadows of the hypothetical future are cast in that significant area to which the various conducive conditions are **mutually** conducive. One can imagine that as the mutual conducives accumulate, what began as a wide-open white screen takes on increasing color, intensifying to saturated chromas in the hues of the final events or outcomes.

A second key question for individual participants is, what is to be your role, not only in the outcome, but in affecting the outcome? Paradigm-shifts, in which everything is in flux, offer extraordinary opportunities for mobility and influence—much greater than when an establishment is firmly in place. So for philanthropists both amateur and professional, and for those who are considering becoming involved in philanthropy in any way (e.g., journalists considering reporting on it), serious questions are raised, of opportunity and responsibility at the strategic level. We shall consider these as well.

To get an overview of this whole situation in philanthropy, and illustrate the practical power of the paradigm-shift analysis, let us compare the Old Paradigm elements with what seems to be emerging as possible New Paradigm counterparts in each of the fundamental categories: Technology, Economy, Institutions, People, Practices, Rhetoric, and Results:

B. The Paradigm-Shift in Philanthropy

Old Paradigm—20th Century	New Paradigm—21st Century?
Technology	
Printing; post-office mail; telephone.	Computerized databases, Internet telecommunications.
Economy	
Traditional diversified 20th-century American—steady growth, generally stable, corporate economy.	"New" high-technology global economy, rapidly expansive, generating huge new wealth from many corporations; old ones merging and acquiring to take advantage of global markets; less local community-oriented.

Old Paradigm—20th Century	New Paradigm—21st Century?
Institutions	
Private foundations lead; Community foundations multiply; Large charities dominate fundraising by direct mail and telemarketing. Professional associations established for grantmakers, fundraisers, and charities; The philanthropic community divides into occupational constituencies. National Taxonomy of Exempt Entities created for research (i.e., not donors).	Donor-advised funds, private foundations multiply; Focus broadens to whole philanthropic community; Barriers dissolve between sectors; Virtual philanthropic communities emerge in cyberspace.
People	
Professionalization makes philanthropy highly technical.	"New and Emerging Donors" (NEDs) explore unconventional modes of giving and volunteering.
Practices	
Industrialized fundraising— telemarketing, direct mail, increasingly competitive grantmaking.	Promoting philanthropy itself; donor education; Venture philanthropy; Giving Circles; E-philanthropy; *Catalogue* systems; Collaborations in and among constituencies and sectors; professional community broadens to include philanthropic advisors, scholars, media.
Rhetoric	
Moral obligation. "Giving away," "Giving Back," through "non-profits" or "tax-exempt entities" in the "third" sector" to the "needy," the "disadvantaged."	Constructive appeal; "Donor-Investors," "making a difference," "social change," "charities" "Philanthropic" or "Benefit" sector; Classical concept of philanthropy as civil education seen as central to American history and character.
Results	
<2% Gross Domestic Product and Adjusted Gross Income; only 25% Itemizers of Charitable Deductions; <20% taxable estates make charitable bequests; 5% largest charities get 80% grant dollars, 80% smallest charities get 5% grant dollars.	Too soon to tell. Aiming much higher.

Several immediate impressions emerge from this arrangement:

1. First, as a check on the chart itself, each of the **two vertical columns "makes sense"**—the items in each respective column seem to fit together, as complementary and relatively coherent **sets** of factors. This tends to confirm that each column represents a distinct, but internally—vertically —coherent, paradigmatic, period of history in philanthropy.

For example, in the first set, a stable and prosperous industrial economy, based on the technology cited and led by successful large national corporations which that technology enables, is consistent with the emergence of that same ideal institutional economies-of-scale model in philanthropy—emulative large national charities, foundations, and professional organizations, developing, promoting, and applying mass-production industrial techniques in their respective activities.

The second set suggests similar vertical correlations: a) a more volatile but ambitious and highly profitable global economy, b) based on high technology, c) producing great wealth in a new set of younger entrepreneurs, d) aggressively innovating with the new tools they learned in business or business schools, and helped develop in the new high-tech economy, e) extending into philanthropy their various individualistic, entrepreneurial approaches to problem-solving and quality-of-life investments, and f) from their great wealth, setting much higher levels of giving.

In both sets, the economy/technology model extends into philanthropy, perhaps because the gifts and grants in philanthropy derive from the characteristic profits made in a given economy. Perhaps "new" economies generate "new" models of philanthropy, accordingly.

2. Second, another self-check: the **mutual incompatibility of each set with the other** strongly suggests that the transition from one to the other is a fundamental paradigm-shift. If that is the case, then the old set is on the way out, the new set is on the way in, and people in the field— both amateurs and professionals —should plan their future involvements accordingly.

3. Third, this arrangement begs the question: does the **side-by-side presentation of the two sets imply horizontal projections and trajectories**, suggesting future directions that are only foreshadowed or implicit at this

stage, but fairly probable? If so, those should be studied and anticipated by planners and strategists. Here are a few suggested trends:

C. Implications

1. Probable Innovations
Some of the bellwether conducive conditions in philanthropy's current paradigm-shift are: **Computerization** and the **Internet** are revolutionalizing all administration and communication, but the revolution is still very much in progress, so detailed outcomes are unpredictable. The **globalization of the economy** will certainly continue, and continue to produce not only unprecedented private wealth, but a corporate infrastructure that will have **cultural and philanthropic ramifications** both here and abroad. The **proliferation of donor-advised funds and new private foundations** will certainly continue, affecting both grantmaking and personal charitable giving. The **blurring and possible dissolution of the boundaries between so-called (false-dichotomy, in philanthropy) "non-profit" and "for-profit" philanthropy and business** will continue, as the technological revolution continues to shuffle and reshuffle the deck; new terminology is called for, but so far none has emerged as paradigmatic for the future. **Systems of donor education and the promotion of philanthropy** will certainly continue to increase and develop, in response to continuing increasing and changing demands. The **acceleration of innovation and experimentation**, which is always characteristic of paradigm-shifts and part of their unpredictability, is another continuing and open-ended development.

2. The Challenged
On the probably losing side of this irreversible fundamental change, certain features of the Old Paradigm now being challenged or ignored will—unless creative adaptations are made—continue to decline in influence. This list is for purposes of illustration only; it is not systematic or comprehensive, but a sampling; suggestive, not definitive; encouraging creativity.

a. *Largest Charities*
Some observers believe that the heyday of large national charities, worthy as they have been and in many cases still are, has come and gone, as technological progress is tending toward decentralization, undermining some (by no means all) of their justifications. Sheer size as a virtue in itself is being qualified by other factors. Some of the large charities once touted as the epitomes of success in philanthropy, seem increasingly like sluggish and faltering dinosaurs, being succeeded in these turbulent times by quicker and nimbler mammals.

The large charities' monopoly of high-cost public visibility, for example, is being superseded by revolutionary, low-cost electronic communications.

The ranges of visibility and accessibility are thus broadening, to include—potentially—the entire sector. Within that broader range, what charities are outstanding will be influenced by other factors than the number of dollars invested in standing-out.

When large size is no longer needed to gain visibility and influence, new rationales are needed to justify the costs of national bureaucratic overhead. Taxing state and local chapters to "support the national" is less compelling or cost-beneficial now than it used to be.

There even seems to be developing a consensus in research that **economies of scale** are not always or automatically valid in the philanthropic sector, for many complex human reasons.

But because most data is still collected by large charities for their own administrative purposes, and because collecting data on small charities is still prohibitively difficult and expensive, there is lag-time between practical knowledge within the fields and academic knowledge of them. Computerization is changing that; computerized data of small charities is much easier and cheaper to collect and analyze; but doing so will take some time yet to develop. One of the problems that will have to be solved is incompatibility and incommensurability of separately conceived and compiled datasets. This is a major issue that we shall also address below.

Innovation and creativity are not generally considered strengths of large charities, and the traditional leading national organizations are in fact not leading today's super-innovative transformation of philanthropy. Fresh ideas and creativity are incubated and nourished more at grassroots levels where problems have to be solved. In large organizations, new ideas have to be conceived and imposed from the top down to retain their freshness; if they originate at the street level, they often have to rise to the top, to the national headquarters, through successive, usually dampening, layers of bureaucratic vetting processes, governed by entrenched interests. It is difficult for people atop large organizations to be free or flexible enough to exercise their imagination, creativity, or openness to outside influences.

b. Largest Traditional Foundations

The Old-Paradigm largest foundations are no longer the largest foundations; they have been joined and in some cases outranked by new peers with different approaches to philanthropy. The upshot is that their traditional social and political position in the philanthropic community is gone. Whether the new cohort will gain similar positions of initiative and leadership, with better ideas and programs, and more dramatic and beneficial strategic capabilities, remains to be seen. Some of the venerable elders are and will be adapting to the new landscape, but undoubtedly many will not, because as privately endowed institutions they have no need to change. Some of them feel incentives to change, others do not. The point is, the traditional largest foundations are no longer setting the agendas for philanthropy as they once did. Whether and to what degree, in what ways, their longer institutional maturity and experience will matter to the future, is not yet clear.

c. National Professional Associations

A number of these organizations have largely and to their credit succeeded in their original missions of professionalizing their constituencies. The sector is now professionalized, and the continuing technical training and certification role has been taken over with far greater productivity and efficiency by undergraduate, graduate, and mid-career training programs for professionals at the local level and on the Internet. Unless the national professional associations reinvent themselves with new strategic missions, they are in danger of having nowhere to go, and some seem to be adrift—their strategic planning efforts have so far have produced meager results. National advocacy (e.g., lobbying Congress) is not an enduring positive role for occupational groups, because few legislative issues affect occupations enough to require their involvement.

Large national conventions attended by thousands began to decline in value even before the Internet, more so since; rising costs of travel, hotels and restaurants in convention centers are further inhibiting. Their fundamental purpose was to enhance communication, but the communications revolution has surpassed them—communications among professionals is now constant, and geographic distance has disappeared as a barrier. National convention agendas must be prepared so far in advance that their content is often stale by the time they occur. Using celebrities to attract attendees is a sign of desperation. Within the professions, web-based communications networks (listserves, etc.) are multiplying so easily, rapidly, and inexpensively, that national-organization networks are preempted and tend to be too broadly gauged.

In particular, "Non-profit" associations are having difficulty because they are mainly fighting the last wars and betting on the wrong horses—focusing on technical training and political advocacy against declining government funding, rather than, say, promoting increased charitable giving or developing fresh ideas about partnerships with government. This is a case where they need to focus on the future, and move into it.

d. Federated Giving Programs

Similarly, **large private federated giving programs** (e.g., United Ways, Community Chests), which were designed for the Old Paradigm and worked well within it, have declined as one after another features of that paradigm's culture, technology, economy, and demographics of giving are being superseded. Workplace giving has faded as younger individual donors increasingly prefer to make their own philanthropic decisions, in family settings. Multinational globalizing corporations have become more deeply engaged abroad—philanthropically as well as industrially and commercially. A small but significant number of highly publicized instances of corruption have damaged certain organizations' reputations. Overhead costs for these fundraising programs are increasingly felt to be burdensome and unnecessary as the Internet encourages direct transactions with charities.

One way out would be for local federated giving programs, as they decline and the national organizations cannot prop them up, to be merged with community foundations; but obviously that is a hard pill to swallow and there are impediments.

An easier and wiser solution might be: a) to broaden out their mission and audience substantially, to include all of philanthropy (not just human services), and b) to turn strategically to focus on donors rather than charities—to promote charitable giving in general, in all fields, providing donor-education services and tools, rather than focusing on their own restricted lists of vetted and approved charities the needs for which are declining. Charitable giving is a growing movement, for which new cost-effective models are emerging. The main reason United Way, for example, focuses on human services is that it was born in the period when "philanthropy" was ill-defined and that is what it meant—before cultural and environmental philanthropy had emerged as significant fields. In short, retooling to adapt to changing times is needed.

e. Industrial Fundraising—Direct-Mail and Telemarketing

Many will cheer to learn that **direct-(postage) mail fundraising** is self-destructing, with assists from its enemies. To the burden of its own offensiveness is now added the communications revolution, which renders it technologically obsolete and cost-ineffective. Electronic alternatives are more economical for everyone, and so more competitive and less profitable; junk mail filters and shields are increasing and increasingly effective, and cold solicitations in a cooler medium are easily clicked into the "Trash." Nonetheless, experiments will continue.

D. Future Trends

A third line of analysis, beyond identifying probably irreversible innovations, and challenges to traditional structures, is to chart some of the trajectories between similar items in the vertical sets, or transitions from Old to New Paradigms, to see if they foreshadow a discernible future:

1. Philanthropy Is Becoming More Fully Visible, Accessible, and Influential

Before the Internet, it was generally impossible for the public or anyone to see, learn and think about, much less strategize about, philanthropy comprehensively—as an organized whole, of significant distinctive parts. We have noted the iceberg phenomenon, that over 90% of charities could not afford broad public visibility through print media; there were other impediments as well.

Because the National Taxonomy of Exempt Entities (NTEE—note the IRS negativism) and its National Center for Charitable Statistics offspring, the "Non-Profit Program Classification System" (NPC—2001) are not systematic in the sense of logically constructed; they portray philanthropy as shapeless and fragmented. Because the word "philanthropy" was indefinite, the phenomenon to which it referred was unclearly perceived, and hardly thought about.

With the Internet, every charity can now afford a public showcase website. Now the only impediment to broad visibility is the challenge of attracting visitors to the sites—of packaging them for public purposes. That is being achieved by collecting those many bits of information in meaningful and practically useful ways—for example, by philanthropic fields of activity in various distinct geographic areas (e.g., philanthropic markets—see Appendix One).

For many and perhaps most **professionals** this may not produce significant change, but for **donors**, it will transform charitable giving by opening up the whole of philanthropy—including whole fields as well as all individual charities—to their consideration. This will go a long way toward leveling the playing field for the vast majority of smaller, highly creative organizations. This in turn should produce endless innovations in how charities relate to the public, to recruit donors and volunteers; how they relate to their actual donors and volunteers; and how they envision and promote themselves and their work to the general public.

Donor education and cultivation are already being significantly enhanced and empowered. How will that develop strategically, in the longer term? Individual charities will always play a limited role, but other entities can and will accomplish much more. The donor-education movement will be strengthened by attracting professionals who are strategically inclined, broadly focused, and intrigued by the potential. Greater visibility will promote greater knowledge and understanding of what philanthropy actually is and how it works. The public media's increasing attention to philanthropy, both at home and abroad, may transform our culture of philanthropy—its role and significance in our lives. Today's *chic* celebrity philanthropy, by magnification in the public media, shows signs of becoming tomorrow's popular movement. If that happens, and philanthropy is correctly understood, America has the possibility of regaining its philanthropic culture.

2. Explosion of Data and Knowledge Management
The computerization of small charities is rapidly expanding their capacities to collect, store, analyze, and use data, which can then be collected and synthesized for strategic purposes throughout philanthropy. This is more powerful than it may seem, especially because knowledge of our field is now so primitive. Most discussions of philanthropy have been either impressionistic (almost always by persons with inadequate practical experience in the sector as a whole), or based on IRS data, whose application to philanthropic practice is crude and misleading. Ignorance and intellectual chaos abound.

What is happening now is that huge new ranges of knowledge about philanthropy are being collected for potential illumination by computerization, the Internet, and search engines. It is only a matter of time before all this is harnessed for practical purposes. Those who take early advantage of these opportunities will flourish.

3. Philanthropy Is Becoming Systematic

If data-collection and data-management continue dramatically to increase in scope and power, where will that lead and/or push philanthropy as a whole?

Practically speaking, the direction depends on where the impetus originates and where it intends to go. If the impetus were coming from traditional national leading institutions, the new knowledge-driven structures would conform to those of the old paradigm and simply extend their power. But that is not the case, perhaps in part because large institutions are slower to innovate, but also because the innovations are spun-off from new-economy start-ups that are many and scattered. What seems actually to be happening is a general efflorescence of knowledge-management innovations, sporadically appearing, coming from and going in all directions at once. At the national level are new institutions like GuideStar, Charity Navigator, Network for Good, and many others. At sub-national levels there are countless new information networks forming in cities, states, and regions, conforming more or less to existing infrastructure and philanthropic "markets," in which donor-investors, charities, and clients, intensify their interactions through new technology.

All this energetic innovation will sort itself out in practice by natural selection, qualified by who provides funding, and for what reasons. Given that: a) in the IT revolution strategically significant funding sources are multiplying and decentralizing, with increasing numbers of new and unconventional private foundations and donor-advised funds; b) also that IT is increasingly powerful in reducing costs; and c) that almost all philanthropy is local; it seems probable that structural and strategic change will be most innovative locally and regionally, pushing out and up to the most practical range and level. Traditional national, monolithic, top-down, programs will collide with innovations coming up from below, producing mutual accommodations.

4. Increasing Use of the Internet as "Participatory Media"

Everyone knows that the Internet and its distinctive forms of electronic communication—e-mail, "Instant Messaging," video-conferencing, blogging, social networking, etc.—are revolutionary, reaching into all corners of our lives in new, expanding, multiplying, ways. Distances in space and time are eliminated as impediments to communication and interaction, to whatever extent and in whatever ways those can occur over the Internet. Information in any form is rapidly being made universally accessible on the Internet. We are headed—no doubt over a period of some time—toward a logical conclusion of universal access to universal information, but no one knows how long that will take, in what order, or in any detail how, or what it will mean for philanthropy or anything else.

One aspect of it all that is strategically significant for philanthropy is its power to engage individuals' participation. Surfing the net is more active than simply reading. Readers can now respond instantaneously to what they read, opening up more energetic dialogues and conversations where there was once largely one-way communications, involving static texts and relatively passive readers in monologues with themselves. Not only are voluntary associations enormously facilitated, and thus empowered, but the ability to interest, to inform, to instruct, to teach, to stimulate, to promote, to advocate, and then to evaluate effectiveness of these communications by inviting and monitoring responses, is vastly increased, which is empowering to all communicators.

5. Donors Organize
Accompanying all these trends are the increasing number and variety of voluntary associations of donors for philanthropic purposes.

Under the Old Paradigm, donors were organized in three ways: by charities, in their own memberships—e.g., associations of alumni, parents, grandparents, or "Friends of" this or that, etc.; by federated giving programs such as Community Chests or United Way, which were often led by prominent corporations exercising corporate citizenship in their communities, organizing their employees for giving and volunteering; and by community foundations, which provided an organized mode of giving for donors in communities where they lived.

Today one of the signs of paradigm-shift is an increasingly widespread and spontaneous movement, especially among high-end or upwardly mobile young donors, to organize themselves for more effective philanthropy, often by specific fields of interest. Donors have formed large ("scalable") voluntary associations for giving, like Social Venture Partners (originally in Seattle and replicated in many cities); or relatively small "giving circles" like the Hestia Fund of Boston, whose 50 members pool their giving for a shared field of interest (e.g., after-school programs for girls); or philanthropic investment clubs. Various donors' clubs have formed like the "50% Club" whose members commit half their incomes to charitable giving.

This phenomenon signifies that philanthropy has become "chic." It bespeaks a yearning for higher aspirations in life-style. It constitutes secular but nonetheless formal declarations of values. It flows into open and hungry spaces in people's lives, perhaps left by declining traditional value-promoting institutions and activities—churches, politics, and formal education. Philanthropy is increasingly being used to teach and promote values, in a period of our history that needs more of them.

6. Philanthropy as a Popular Movement

Where all this is leading is less knowable. It is one thing to identify current developments, on the basis of evidence. It is another to infer which among those signify trends, and to identify them accurately; that is historical judgment—based on knowledge and insight, informed by experience. The next step, even further removed from evidence, would be to hypothesize where those inferred trends will lead; that can only be speculation. There is nothing wrong with it, so long as everyone understands that this discussion is hypothetical—no more, no less.

To summarize: we have noted that 1) computer and Internet information and communications technology is making philanthropy more fully visible to the general public; 2) the increase of data, and of its management will continue to accelerate rapidly; 3) this process will illuminate fields and subfields of philanthropy, to unprecedented degrees and in new ways, for donors, grantmakers and strategists; 4) this will inevitably make philanthropy more systematic and strategic, significantly increasing productivity and efficiency; 5) the new information and communications technology will significantly increase fundraising and charitable giving; 6) the Internet's development as a participatory medium will significantly empower communication and promotion of philanthropic opportunities, as well as evaluation of responses through various feedback mechanisms; 7) while all this is going on, donors will continue to organize, in new and innovative ways for more effective and satisfying participation in philanthropy.

From all this it is clear that in this current paradigm-shift, philanthropy is gaining momentum. In the last ten years the word itself has become common parlance. More and more attention is being paid to it in the media, including the blogosphere. As more is known, and thought, and communicated, about it, by more people and in more institutions, philanthropy is developing the capacity to become a popular cultural movement.

We noted in Chapter II, that all movements in American history begin as philanthropy—"private initiatives for public good, focusing on quality of life." The American Revolution itself, anti-slavery, women's suffrage and feminism, conservation and environmentalism, prohibition and civil rights, all began as private initiatives aimed at becoming political movements that would change laws and even the Constitution. That they aimed at and ultimately found expression in politics does not detract from the fact that they began as private philanthropic initiatives. That is how American democracy—which itself began as philanthropy—works. The Classical Greek tag, "philanthropic and democratic" is a bonded pair in relatively free societies.

But what does it mean that philanthropy **itself** has the potential to become, and now shows signs of actually becoming, a popular movement? For a start, it means that Americans are increasingly inclined, privately and voluntarily, to assume public or civic responsibilities—one of philanthropy's slogans is, "If you see something that needs doing, do it!"

Much has been written in recent decades about declines in voting participation, public apathy, dropping out, "Me generations," and other symptoms of social alienation. Perhaps those trends are beginning to be reversed by increasing philanthropy?

If traditional custodians of values in our society—churches, fraternal organizations, schools, the courts, politics, even families—have declining influence on our people and especially our youth; and if philanthropy is becoming more popular, is it possible that philanthropy now—fully illuminated and powerfully teaching—has the potential to become our school for values?

In this context, it is especially significant that the kind of philanthropy which is in the ascendant is not that of the Old Paradigm—technically and procedurally robust, but substantively narrow—rich people helping poor people, out of a sense of moral obligation or duty. If the future of philanthropy is in the Classical, humane, educational, conceptually clear, tradition, it will promote humane self-development in both benefactors and beneficiaries.

It makes a certain sense that, when all else fails—when our great social, cultural, and political institutions and systems lose their capacities for leadership—we are by default thrown back at last on ourselves, as individuals and families, to stand for something. We are our own last resort. How fortunate (not to say miraculous) it is that at just this moment in our history, technologically-empowered philanthropy emerges as a cultural influence, moving towards the center from the periphery of our social consciousness and personal lifestyles!

What that suggests is that Americans, and especially American donors, should feel some urgency about investing in donor education and the promotion of philanthropy itself—**private** initiatives, public **good**, and **quality** of life.

7. A Note on the Globalization of American Philanthropy

"The world" is very rapidly changing. Actually we are in the period of the largest (and growing), fastest (and accelerating) change in all of human history, powered by the accelerating development of modern technology itself. The triumph of capitalism, science, and technology, as a mutually-reinforcing and -empowering system, will in the 21st century transform the human condition, for better or worse. We cannot predict which it will be, because the challenges we face pose greater, more profound and more difficult strategic problems than the human race as a whole has ever confronted—e.g., harnessing and transferring our energy reliance from non-renewable to sustainable sources; resolving polarities of wealth and poverty; eradicating diseases and neutralizing disabilities; promoting education and training for this new scientific-technological capitalist system worldwide; stabilizing our environmental relations for long-term sustainability; and resolving the fundamental cultural confrontations of science with traditional religions.

In this challenging and even daunting context, what will be the roles and potentials of philanthropy?

There is already a sizable and admirable technical literature on the globalization of philanthropy—how, where and why it is growing, what kinds of institutions and practices are or are not working well, issues in developing viable relations with governments and other established authorities, challenges of fundraising in various cultures and economies, etc. On the whole, the picture is extremely various and volatile, in a rapid-growth scenario. No single paradigm either exists or appears to be emerging yet, though it is certain that whatever emerges from the paradigm-shift in America will powerfully inform the future of global philanthropy and even of world history. Many of the trends we have noted above are already moving around the world.

This book is especially concerned with cultural and historical issues: with the Classical tradition, its rebirth in the Renaissance and Enlightenment, and its transplantation to America in the Colonial and Revolutionary periods, its neglect in the late-twentieth century paradigm, and its possible re-emergence in the current American paradigm-shift.

We have especially noted how American philanthropy arose during the Colonial period, to become an essential force in the American Revolution, to the point that Alexis de Tocqueville cited its "voluntary associations" as a cardinal feature and expression of the American character, distinguishing us from the Old World national cultures, which were accordingly less hospitable to democracy. This continued and strengthened the intimate associations of Classical philanthropy with freedom and democracy, and liberal education.

All cultures value giving by the rich to the poor. To promote increased giving on that model is beneficial, especially as economies develop and the numbers of rich and the scale of their wealth increase. Americans are known to be the most generous people on Earth, so promoting generosity—the ratio of giving to having—is significant.

Far more profound would be the globalization of Classical American philanthropy—the kind that launched this nation, that produced the American Revolution, that was ultimately derived from the great Western Classical, philosophical, tradition of philanthropy.

Classical philanthropy took root here because we had a unique historical situation—nation-building from scratch, in bounteous circumstances, during the Enlightenment. Our culture of philanthropy then was a practical necessity, which eventually found political expression in a democratic revolution, seeking freedom from a perceived tyrannical foreign government. Other nations of the world today do not have our historical and environmental blessings, but the globalization of American philanthropy will not be simply a matter of disseminating our institutional models and practices abroad. The globalization of American philanthropy will be a powerful force and training-ground for freedom and democracy.

If Americans today find that our nation's foreign policy leaves something to be desired, we might consider that through philanthropy, every American can have a foreign policy. Do you believe that women in the Middle East should be educated? That children should be given computers? That HIV/AIDS must be stopped? That the world's biodiversity should not be sacrificed to short-term exploitation of natural resources? No matter what your concerns are, you can magnify your influence worldwide through philanthropy. Think what that would do for our image and influence in the world!

V. Philanthropy Reborn

The argument of the previous four chapters has hypothetical, practical ramifications for everyone in philanthropy.

The concept of "rebirth" has a long and distinguished tradition in Western cultural history. The "Renaissance" in early modern times, was the first historical period named by contemporaries, because they thought that's what was happening culturally. They and many others in the Christian tradition even today have also used the doctrine of rebirth (being "born again"), signifying a new life, or a fresh start in life. The essence of the idea is that, whether in history or in life, a return to beginnings can produce a renewal of life and vigor that we associate with youth—which is as refreshing for cultures as it is for people. A return of philanthropy to its Classical origins would be reviving, refreshing, re-energizing and reinforcing.

The strong connection between Classical philanthropy, democracy and freedom, repeated at our birth as a nation, suggests that re-invigorating philanthropy with its Classical mode would also re-invigorate America and our democracy—a return to our roots, that once made this nation great and of such great promise in world history. Just as it brought out the best in our Founders, it would also bring out the best in us as Americans, and in America as a philanthropic nation, purportedly beneficial for all mankind. This, as we said above, adds the "inducements of patriotism" to those of philanthropy.

Two questions for philanthropists are: how should each of us negotiate the fundamental changes and turmoil of the paradigm-shift, and what are our likely futures in the New Paradigm? There are a few general strategies to consider:

First, we would do well to relax our holds on the Old Paradigm (or its hold on us), and let go of it altogether as soon as we see viable new futures for ourselves or our institutions. In a period of rapid, fundamental, structural and strategic change, timing is critical for survival, and innovation is actually safer than obsolescence. The future is unfolding rapidly, and being left behind is disadvantageous. It is appropriate, and actually advisable now, to experiment with innovations of our own, to find our new niches—increasing numbers of colleagues are experimenting with the new technology, for example. Not all the experiments being tried these days will succeed, but in an age of innovation there is no shame and little danger in trying various possibilities. Managers of institutions especially should avoid clinging to traditional ways as if they were life-rafts, because they may be the opposite, dragging us under. They will slow our development and we may one day find it too late to change. We should embrace the future, and waste no time on nostalgia.

Second, collaboration, not competition, is the spirit of the new philanthropy. We should take a tip from the Stoics and others, and adopt as a working principle that in philanthropy we are all on the same team, and in our communities it is the home team. We are all one body—all are members, one of another. We each have different gifts, and we should use them, in harmony, and explore their interdependencies. Collaboration is one of our characteristic distinctions from business which we share with government at its best, in part because we are always working with volunteers, so we need to cultivate a welcoming working atmosphere. Philanthropy is not a zero-sum game with either the dollar or power as a bottom line. We are all exercising our "private initiatives for public good, focusing on quality of life," so if we see opportunities for collaboration, we should take advantage of them because it will make all partners more effective.

Third, if philanthropy is continuing education, we are all teachers and students. Education, or self-development, obviously starts early and ends late, actually with our bequests. Each of us will benefit by considering what it is we are teaching those around us by our examples. We all will benefit from cultivating our humanity.

Various constituencies of philanthropy might consider these particular inferences:

A. Donors

Charitable giving in the Old Paradigm was too technical and negative—giving away, giving back, to non-profit, non-governmental, tax-exempt, organizations, in the third (out of three) sectors, for the disadvantaged, the "have-nots," etc. Given these uninspiring, monotonous words and ideas, the rhetoric persuading donors to act on them was about moral obligation, which tended to guilt-trip the rich. The New Paradigm is more constructive—loving humanity, self-development, making the world a better place, investing in quality of life—about opportunities, not obligations.

The Old Paradigm focused on procedural and technical issues—ways and means; the New Paradigm is more about substance and content, results and their significance—what philanthropy means, positively, for both benefactors and beneficiaries.

These differences help explain why the paradigm is shifting.

Loving humanity naturally begins with one's own humanity. Here we are not talking about being in love with ourselves, but about loving—in the sense of caring for, respecting, honoring, helping, cultivating, nurturing, and developing—what makes us human: all the personal talents, abilities, resources, attributes, characteristics, and strengths, that make us what we are as **human** beings. (We mean no disrespect to other animals.)

The purpose of philanthropy is to develop all these attributes, in ourselves and our beneficiaries, to their fullest, so that we all become more fully humane—all that we can be as humans, striving for excellence in our own self-development. Our hearts and our brains are vital, sensory, organs and instruments; in philanthropy we cultivate and learn to rely on them. We teach ourselves; we are in charge of our own liberal education. This is a life-long process, the deepest and fullest "continuing education."

Philanthropy helps us in this central mission of life, not by telling us what our values should be, but by inviting us to identify our own values—not just to talk about them, but to exercise them, through active, self-initiated, self-propelled, meaningful, benefactions: charitable giving and volunteering.

By exercising our values, they become stronger and more refined. The experience teaches us how good they are, how well they work in practice, how they might be enhanced and improved. By increasing our knowledge and understanding of our own values, and skill in our capabilities, we grow.

Moreover, by identifying our values—what we care about—we are in effect identifying, defining, ourselves: who we are, what kinds of people we are, what we care about enough to act on. No matter who we are—no matter how idiosyncratic our tastes and values, there are charities just like us, that we will enjoy supporting **because** they are just like us. In this way also, philanthropy extends and increases ourselves and our personal influences.

All this is why, if philanthropy becomes a popular movement, it has a serious shot at becoming our nation's school for values in this secular age and culture—just as it was in the 18th-century Enlightenment. Now, as then, this is true because there is a lack of serious competition. Then the culture was coming out of disorderly religion; today we are coming out of unhealthy secularity and its fragmentation of life. In both cases, hunger for moral and even spiritual nourishment evokes value-intensive living. Philanthropy is good, and good for us.

B. Trustees

Trustees are already, *ex officio*, donors and volunteers. Everything just said applies especially to them as well—and more. In addition to their legal responsibilities spelled out in detail in both statutes and their institutions' by-laws, which are beyond the scope of this book, there are several dimensions of their work that should be noted here.

I prefer the designation "trustee" over "director," to emphasize a fact often ignored or neglected: that the core of their responsibilities is to represent the public interest in these privileged (tax-exempt, tax-incentived) corporations. This is a public trust—in the moral rather than the legalistic sense. They are entrusted by the public to ensure that the public interest, for which the corporation was granted its privileged status, is indeed well-served—that its mission is being responsibly fulfilled, and that no private profit is being improperly derived from its funds and activities.

Only one of the trustees is truly a "Director," and that is the "Executive Director," who should be a full voting member of the Board of Trustees, *ex officio*—on account of his or her office. The Trustees' proper role is governance, not management. The Executive Director should be the chief executive officer of the corporation, reporting to the Board of Trustees as a whole, obviously recusing him/herself from discussions and votes affecting his/her contract, but otherwise fully participatory as an equal Trustee of the public interest in the corporation, meriting the support of fellow Trustees in carrying out the policies, plans and fiscal allocations proposed by the professional staff and authorized or set by the Board as a whole.

For these reasons, under the New Paradigm, Trustees and Executive Directors have potentially at least an educational responsibility and function. At the interface between the corporation and the public, they should also teach the public the values of both the corporation and of philanthropy itself, of which the corporation is a particular example. They should also teach the corporation, its staff and beneficiaries, the public philanthropic interest in what they are all doing together.

Teaching requires knowledge, understanding, and persuasive articulation. That is how trustees help build support for, and further enable, the institution. Therefore one of their main tasks is to learn about, appreciate, and practice teaching about, philanthropy in general and their institution in particular. This is more about outreach than in-reach—learning all about the programs and staff of the institution, but for purposes of outreach to other institutions and people that may help the institution grow and prosper in its mission.

C. Grantmakers

That the paradigm-shift in philanthropy is caused by technological transformation means that data and its management systems are rapidly and dramatically improving, increasing the power to make better, more strategic and cost-effective, grants.

For grantmakers, the enormous increase in manageable data means that philanthropy is on the verge of becoming systematic. The *Catalogue for Philanthropy's* system of on-line *Directories* in Massachusetts (see Appendix One) is the first to illuminate the entire sector—not just all charities, but all fields, systematically organized individually and collectively by a comprehensive typology and a single, logical, stable, and user-friendly, taxonomy of fields, fully mappable, chartable and analyzable in terms of various parameters, in various combinations. Because this development is driven by technological advance, it will multiply.

Community foundations (CFs), for example, will be able to map and chart their community's entire philanthropic resources—what charities exist and how they relate to each other; what services they provide and how those interrelate; what resources they bring to the table, how those are distributed and interrelated across the community; and also what resources are lacking that are needed, what charities are available nearby to provide them, what that will cost. CFs will be able to have "field development programs," in which they convene heads of all charities in each field or combinations of fields in their regions, show them how resources are distributed, find out how needs are distributed, and together in the presence of donors and other grantmakers, tackle the structural and strategic issues of their communities' quality of life. This has never been possible to do systematically or completely; it will become routine, for many community foundations, as a substantial service to the whole community and its philanthropy.

It is quite possible that the New Paradigm will enable CFs to come into their own as philanthropic resources, promoting philanthropy as such, and building philanthropic capacity, at the community level, through donor education (friendraising), fundraising and grantmaking. The Old Paradigm organized philanthropy in national professional associations—grantmakers, fundraisers, executive directors, volunteer-managers, and their sub-groups. In an age of professionalization and growth, that made sense. Now that professionalization is complete, and technical training programs abound in other institutions and on the Internet, philanthropy is being re-organized, with new rationales. The option most obvious to us at the *Catalogue*, which we have reinforced for Massachusetts and are instituting on our website, and distributing to other philanthropic markets, is to organize philanthropy at the local community level, around community foundations that actively promote philanthropy as such, in its entirety.

The *Catalogue*'s system of *Directories* identifies and maps every CF's service area, associates every charity with its CF, and refers users to the CFs as a reference for them to help identify and vet charities of their interest. This is explicitly an effort to strengthen the role of CFs in the philanthropic infrastructure, and in particular their role as promoters of philanthropy at the local level. It makes far more practical sense to organize philanthropy around the more than 700 CFs than in terms of a relatively few national associations of professions or kinds of institutions. While many and perhaps most CFs are not equipped now to bear this responsibility fully, the tools are now available, with the *Catalogue*'s *Directories* system, for them to grow into their proper and much stronger role as the mainstays of the emerging subfield of philanthropy: promoting philanthropy.

New family foundations are multiplying rapidly in the New Paradigm economy—half of all foundations in 2008 are less than ten years old—and for them the new conditions in philanthropy are also dramatically improving. First, with new Internet-based tools like FoundationSource and the *Catalogue* system, creating and operating a foundation—institutionalizing personal and family philanthropy—is easier, more economical, and more philanthropically effective, than ever, which should mean that these institutions will also increase and improve, and become much more satisfying than ever in personal and family lifestyles. The *Catalogue's* web-based *Directories* system especially makes it possible for new foundations to identify their philanthropic niches more readily, with greater confidence, control, and discipline, with all of philanthropy at their disposal—not just what they or someone they happen to know, happens to know, at the outset. Greater ease and interest in the new Internet-based methods of scoping-out fields and the sector as a whole will attract younger family members as well, making it possible for them to discover and navigate their philanthropic opportunities with greater confidence and productivity than ever, as they mature.

Traditional, Old-Paradigm, foundations have some fateful fork-in-the-road decisions to make. On the one hand, because they are endowed institutions, they don't have to change unless they want to, so for them the argument of this book poses that question: Given the changing world around you, do you want to change as well? As the shift continues, the reasons to change will become increasingly clear and persuasive, so one option is just to sit tight and observe closely. If, at a minimum, a traditional foundation decides formally to consider changing its own paradigm, there are plenty of tools and advisors available to assist them. They might commission a study of their own options and potential results. Or, in a broader community spirit, they might commission one or more studies of the issues raised generally by the paradigm-shift—what are the foreseeable impacts of the paradigm-shift on the various fields of their traditional interests, what structural and strategic issues ought they to consider for the future. Or, taking a more pro-active role, they might conclude that a paradigm-shift is indeed occurring around them, and decide to facilitate it or certain parts of it through precisely-targeted grants.

Paradigm-shifts offer the greatest opportunities for historical influence, because everything is in flux; when things are already in motion, one has only to nudge them to modify their direction. An example is the Ellis L. Phillips Foundation, which originated the *Catalogue for Philanthropy*. As a small (endowment below $5 million) family foundation, they achieved nationwide influence on philanthropy as a whole, merely by a few experiments in Massachusetts. The greatest leverage a foundation can achieve is to promote philanthropy itself—multiplying rather than adding to philanthropy, by grants that leverage the resources of others in desired directions. Foundations might well consider establishing *Catalogue* systems in their communities—the *Catalogue* has already developed the tools with which to accomplish this easily and inexpensively, to the great benefit of local philanthropic communities.

In sum, philanthropic foundations are now being presented with new tools that can help them be more strategic in their grantmaking, especially with respect to investing in whole groups of charities or even fields of philanthropy. Grantmaking programs are traditionally organized by fields; with the new tools, grantmakers can tailor their grants to shape those entire fields, or indeed the entire sector locally, for the future. The point is, whatever choice is made at this exciting time in the history of philanthropy, the best strategy is to move into the future of philanthropy facing forward, not backward.

D. Philanthropic Advisors

Philanthropic advising is a relatively young field, and was itself an early indicator of the paradigm-shift, because it arose in response to increasing needs for assistance on the part of the "new and emerging donors"—often relatively young, major donors and grant-makers who were and are a powerful force for paradigm-shift.

The strengths of philanthropic advisors are their personal devotion to philanthropy, often acquired by experience, often from their own family backgrounds, or even previous professional grantmaking. Usually where they themselves need help is in detailed knowledge of the field as a whole, and of broad ranges within it. Ignorance is not their fault, given the paucity of teaching tools provided under the Old Paradigm. One of the greatest strengths of the paradigm-shift, however, is in rapidly expanding data and knowledge of the whole, and of its parts in that context. Given these tools, philanthropic advisors can flourish.

We might offer two suggestions: get to know the new teaching tools, and help develop and disseminate them. Ride the crest of the wave by developing your own expertise in the rapidly developing donor-education tools market. Persuade your clients to help support the development of these new technologies and resources in your local area and beyond. Move the ball downfield, be a leader in your community and recognized as such.

E. Financial Service Providers, Attorneys, and Accountants

Money managers, attorneys and accountants are increasingly called upon, or find opportunities, to provide philanthropic advice and services for wealthy clients and their families. Surveys show that under the Old Paradigm, technical and negative language and moralistic rhetoric have made it awkward for financial advisors to advocate philanthropy, because "non-profit" moralistic considerations conflict with for-profit technical discussions.

The New Paradigm eliminates that conflict of interest, replacing it with a harmony of interest between investments for personal and economic quality of life, and for personal and community quality of life. In the New Paradigm, philanthropic investments are seen as a natural extension of financial investments. Many of the same considerations—due diligence, cost-benefit ratios, balanced and broadly distributed portfolios, etc.—apply, and value is added, by the extension. Here the financial advisor may well contribute skilled suggestions, especially if assisted by philanthropic investment tools such as the *Directories* system, which provide complete information and facilitate analyses of available philanthropic investment opportunities.

Or to put it another way: under the Old Paradigm, introducing philanthropy into a discussion with a client was to change the subject diametrically, from profit to non-profit, from technical to moralistic. The New Paradigm not only eliminates the contradictions, but provides a convenient bridge from one to the next—both discussions being about investments and quality of life. Both are about maximizing returns on investments; the difference between them has to do with the nature of the returns. Philanthropic returns are non-material, however the client sees them—as psychic, life-enhancing, family-enhancing, spiritual, or simply the pleasure and satisfaction of making a beneficial difference in the world.

F. Fundraisers

1. Problems Within the Old Paradigm
In the last half of the twentieth century, fundraising was about raising money for the fundraiser's employer or client—one charity at a time. The vocabulary (words), conceptualization (ideas) and rhetoric (appeal to donors) tended to be technical and negative. Fundraisers, at the interface between charities and the donating public, were the sales force. Fundraising was selling; its effectiveness was measured impersonally, in dollars alone.

This is what gave Old-Paradigm fundraising its image problem, indicated by the transparently cosmetic names of the two main professional associations: the "American Association of Fundraising **Counsel**" (AAFRC) and the "National Society of Fund Raising **Executives**" (NSFRE), and its successor, the "Association of Fundraising **Professionals**" (AFP). Also for cosmetic reasons, one of the two main purposes of NSFRE was "certification," and members were urged and expected to add the credentialing initials "CFRE" (Certified Fund Raising Executive") after their names in professional functions. (AFP has divorced itself from the certification program.) Part of the purpose of certification, of course, was to distinguish between the noble and the ignoble, who evidently were lurking around.

Donors and grantmakers, the objects of fundraisers' attentions, were certainly aware of these problems. People do not look forward serenely to encounters with salesmen, especially when they can expect being made to feel morally obliged to say yes. Grantmakers and some donors have felt morally as well as technically obliged to look under the hood, to kick the tires, to exercise "due diligence" and above all not to trust what they are told, because at bottom the encounter is set up to be in some ways, to some extent, implicitly adversarial and manipulative—to get the donor to give away or give back, something many people feel may not be entirely in their self-interest—especially when the fundraiser's job performance and professional stature is going to be measured in terms of dollars raised, rather than, say, in donor satisfaction.

It is no wonder, in this context, that fundraisers have tended to become mercenary technicians—with high turnover, chasing ever-higher salaries, especially in comparison with colleagues in program, management, or even leadership, positions. Nor is it hard to see why, in this context, the results in funds raised were not so great after all (flat for a half-century at ca. 2% GDP), or why *Giving USA* (published until recently by AAFRC) consistently reported the results as a success story.

2. New Paradigm Solutions
The New Paradigm offers transforming opportunities for fundraisers and the fundraising profession. If they adopt the Classical view of philanthropy as education and humane self-development, fundraisers—at the interface between philanthropy and donors or grantmakers—become the faculty rather than the sales staff, and for philanthropy rather than their individual employers. This single, basic, adjustment eliminates the image problems,

uplifts the vocabulary, conceptualization and rhetoric of the profession, and the profession itself, to edifying and inspiring levels, and—surprisingly perhaps—improves results in **both** fundraising and friendraising.

In the New Paradigm, relations between fundraisers and donors become collegial, rather than adversarial—as members of the same team, of co-philanthropists—one professional, one amateur. The job of the fundraiser is as a philanthropic advisor, helping donors to be better philanthropists, to gain more satisfaction and personal fulfillment from philanthropy as a lifestyle. The subject of their conversations is automatically focused where it should be in effective fundraising: on the donor and what the donor wants, on this and other charitable investment opportunities, and on helping the donor get involved with public issues about which the donor is concerned. In this the fundraiser is also a philanthropist, loving the human development of the donor. The idealism provides a spacious and ennobling framework: the Classical tradition of education, culture, and civilization; for religious persons, in the love of God; for Americans, in joining a patriotic tradition that is quintessentially American, and enhancing our quality of life in America.

Relations with grantmakers become similarly collegial, collaborating professionally as members of the same team to make the best, most cost-effective, use of dollars already dedicated to the philanthropic purposes of the donor and board.

The tenor of the discussion becomes positive, constructive, and clearly—indeed emphatically—idealistic. It is primarily about investing in the public good, on what the gift will accomplish objectively for good; and secondarily about the subjective personal growth and professional satisfaction that will result from making the world a better place and from empowering and enhancing the humanity of others. In this discussion donor skepticism and cynicism do not arise, because there is no incentive, and far greater difficulty, for the fundraiser to deceive the donor, when the subject is the donor, more than just the dollars. Moreover, in a culture of authentic philanthropy, inauthentic pseudo-philanthropy is easier to detect because it stands out more conspicuously, as a blemish.

In this process, the appropriate measure of success is donor-satisfaction—in the relation of dollars, their results, and the donors, in both fundraising and friend-raising. The subject is not just the charities involved, but philanthropy itself in both donors and beneficiaries. A rising tide lifts all boats; everyone in philanthropic fundraising should be focused on the tide, not just the boats as in the Old Paradigm. Experience shows that grateful donors are more generous; fundraisers who have chosen this path have seen their results improve. The best, surest, way to increase charitable giving is through donor education—strengthening the culture of philanthropy.

G. Leaders and Managers of Charities

Over 90% of Executive Directors (EDs) are leading and managing relatively young and small charities, which usually cannot afford full-time professional staff in such institution-development tasks as fundraising and public relations. Most EDs are also program-oriented professionals, many of whom conceived and founded the charities they lead and manage; their highest priority, and often greatest skill, is not institution-development, but program effectiveness. They are all overworked and underpaid, and very often serve their causes at some personal sacrifice. Considering the challenges and adversities of small-charity management and development, they are the most skillful, practical, resourceful, managers and leaders in philanthropy; they do more with less than the small minority who have managed to work their way into larger institutions, and they deserve enormous philanthropic respect. This is a considered judgment, based on 25 years' deep, detailed, and extensive experience with this constituency. They have been the central focus of the Massachusetts *Catalogue for Philanthropy* for the last twelve years, during which we have evaluated and worked with thousands of individuals and individual organizations, in all fields, all across one of the largest states in the nation. We can therefore say authoritatively that they constitute a marvelous resource of sensitivity, intelligence, creativity, talent, skills, and sheer benefaction for quality of life in society.

This is not to detract in any way from the EDs of larger charities, who are more likely to be skilled institution-builders and leaders in broader arenas. A recent large national survey found that leaders in philanthropy are more competent and highly regarded as **leaders** than their counterparts in business (the most amusing finding was that business CEOs think more highly of themselves than either their staffs or their competitors do, while charity CEOs' self-evaluations are realistic—consistent with the judgments of their staffs and peers).

Therefore any suggestion that philanthropic leaders and managers are less competent than in business or government is, in my experience and to put it politely, uninformed. People coming into philanthropy from the other sectors should approach with respect and in a spirit of inquiry, rather than with condescension. Apparent comparative lacks of management techniques and resources are functions of an economy of scarcity in philanthropy generally, of not being able to afford them, given the higher commitment to and urgency of investing in programs than in overhead.

How then should EDs respond to the paradigm-shift now occurring in philanthropy? First, it would be wise to strengthen their institutions' reliance on individual donors for financial support. Many EDs automatically think of corporate and foundation grants as their primary funding source—this despite the fact that in round numbers, corporations provide only 5% of private dollars in philanthropy, foundations only 10%; individuals' annual giving provides roughly 70%, their bequests 15%. Government support is fickle and has been generally declining for several decades. So although private and public institutional grantmakers are easier to find and identify as prospective funders, and extremely valuable for new projects or programs, and with larger charities, they are not suitable for long-term reliance by most organizations. For sustainability, strong follow-through will be needed from individual giving and loyal personal supporters.

Fortunately, personal giving is, and in the New Paradigm will continue to be, increasing, so charities are well-advised to develop that growing resource as their primary sustainable revenue. Charities and their leaders should add promoting philanthropy to their central activities and ideas, developing ways to teach the values of philanthropy in lifestyles, rather than just selling their own organizations all the time. They can easily create informal occasions when the subject is philanthropy, not themselves, and they can collaborate with community foundations to do so.

These days there is much discussion about the importation into philanthropy of venture-capital practices and values. Much of it is beneficial—"due diligence," quantification, Management by Objectives—though none of these is new in philanthropy, contrary to general impressions. Some of it however is not beneficial—e.g., a spirit of competition among charities for fundraising dollars, which is inappropriate in philanthropy, and predicated on a false assumption that the search for philanthropic funding is a zero-sum game (when giving is growing).

The New Paradigm will almost certainly increase philanthropic engagement in our society, and in particular charitable giving and volunteering. Helping to make this happen should be a high priority for leaders and managers of charities in every field.

Promoting Philanthropy is a newly-designated field, at the donor-friendly interface between philanthropy as a whole and the donating/volunteering public as a whole. It includes the over 700 Community Foundations, though they are not yet generally aware of it as their mission. The New Paradigm will strengthen it further, through donor education and the provision of tools to help donors.

International philanthropy will also be strengthened because these charities will be more visible and accessible, and can be more easily vetted, with current technology. Its rationale is substantially enhanced by the Classical view of philanthropy as a promoter of democracy and freedom. The same factors that are pushing the paradigm-shift—technological revolution, the globalization of the American economy, and changed demographics of wealth—are producing cosmopolitan wealth-creators as the leading wave of new donors for the future. If every American major donor had a foreign policy, expressed through their international philanthropy, what a difference that would make!

H. New Professionals

This is a great time to enter the profession or to work in it, because the atmosphere is bracing and dynamic, problematic issues are being constructively resolved, and the future for philanthropy is bright. Many folks in mid-careers elsewhere are now moving into philanthropy for greater personal and professional satisfaction, which is surely a good and healthy sign, and evidence that it is true and that media attention is making positive impressions. Many more young people are seeking graduate training in "public administration" and M.B.A. curricula with emphases on philanthropic institutions and practices, and their idealism is palpable.

The first advice for these folks is to notice that a paradigm-shift is in progress. This has several ramifications.

One is that they need to be planning for the future, not the past. This means that they should scope out their own situation and options, being careful to avoid the Old Paradigm, and if possible finding a suitable and exciting New Paradigm opportunity.

Another is that professional options in philanthropy are rapidly expanding. Many innovative experiments are happening, and it is advantageous for newcomers to discover and explore as many of those as possible, to consider first whether any of them might be right for themselves.

Finally, more than ever before, one of those options to be carefully considered is carving out a new niche for oneself, custom-designed to fit one's own unique set of talents, knowledge, skills and resources, rather than simply joining traditional positions and career paths. New needs and possibilities are constantly emerging now, and for many there is no established resource in place. So here as always in philanthropy we say, "If you see something that needs doing, do it!"

I. Scholars

It is not in any way disrespectful to observe, as a former Renaissance historian and faculty dean, that as matters of demonstrable fact, scholarship in the field of philanthropic studies is still in its infancy, and generally not read or followed by professionals in the field. These conditions are interrelated. Scholarship in philanthropic studies is hardy, worthy, and respectable; scholars have in most cases come to their subjects from other disciplines, so that their intellectual contexts and references have been naturally informed more by, and often aimed more at, those disciplines, academic departments, journals, and colleagues, than by and at their new practice and profession of philanthropy. "Philanthropic Studies" is not yet a commonly recognized academic subject and discipline, and there is considerable questioning as to whether it should become such. In this context we offer five suggestions, informed by the paradigm-shift: 1) to tighten up the language and conceptualization of the field, 2) to move beyond IRS categories in refining its data, 3) to sharpen its focus for New Paradigm research by considering what we have called the Classical view of philanthropy, 4) to identify clearly and appropriately the audiences and purposes of this field of scholarship, in accordance with the New Paradigm, and 5) to ensure that curricula address these issues, to prepare students adequately for the future of philanthropy.

1. **Language:** Basic terminology—"philanthropy," "non-profit," "volunteer" and their cognates, need to be sorted out rigorously. In the New Paradigm, the IRS lexicon is expansively beside the point. The profit/non-profit distinction is a false dichotomy in practical philanthropy, which is increasingly practiced by both types of institutions. "Non-profit" is far from defining philanthropy, even if it weren't a misnomer anyway, outside the IRS. No mature intellectual or scientific discipline tolerates such loose language, and to do so is regarded from rigorously scholarly and scientific perspectives— someone has to say it, regretfully—a veritable badge of technical immaturity. Fortunately the English language is more than adequately equipped to serve scholarly purposes in philanthropy; all it takes is work, to make it work.

2. Data: While it is understandable that we have relied on IRS data heretofore, because it has been the largest, cheapest, dataset available, technology now enables us to transcend its shortcomings. The IRS numbers of "non-profits" include so many institutions outside philanthropy as normally conceived and practiced, that they are very misleading to donors, grantmakers and strategists. Even within any reasonable definition of "philanthropy," a basic typology such as the one suggested in Appendix One is needed to clarify our thought and practice. The National Taxonomy of fields is intellectually chaotic, and because its field designations are not logically coherent, it is technically not a taxonomy at all, not navigable by donors, not suited for donor education, and not couched in terms donors use. Scholarship begins with sound data; philanthropic studies need to establish and validate theirs.

3. Focus: The Classical concept of philanthropy, as either educational ideal or type of character, is elusive as a subject of scholarship outside the history of ideas. As an objective behavioral act, "private initiatives for public good, focusing on quality of life" is not likely to be a major issue, though it can be identified and studied, and its episodes are likely to be more significant historically than its traditional counterparts of "rich people helping poor people," or "caring," or "giving." When such behaviors are institutionalized, as for example in voluntary associations or charitable institutions, their history and typologies become suitable subjects for scholarly research, as well as significant historically and in the social-scientific disciplines. To re-orient philanthropic studies around the Classical tradition of philanthropy in thought and practice, would be intellectually rewarding and strategically both practical and wise, as we hope to have demonstrated in Chapter II, above. By so enlarging the subject in content and significance, the influence and prestige of the discipline will increase.

4. Purposes: The primary function and responsibility of this field of scholarship in the New Paradigm will be to enhance the practice of philanthropy by professionals and amateurs alike, which will be crucially important not just to the field itself, but also to our culture and society. This practical and cultural, rather than technically academic, orientation will enrich the field intellectually, and increase its general influence both within and outside academe. In the New Paradigm, scholars in philanthropic studies will have a much more influential and respectable role to play than ever before, if only they will accept it.

5. Curricula: Scholars in Philanthropic Studies who are teaching graduates or undergraduates these days need to teach to the future, not the past—

especially if they wish to compete effectively for students and funding. Their curricula should be evaluated as to adequacy in addressing the future. Are there courses, or sections of courses, on the paradigm-shift? Are there, built into curricula and courses, the subjects of the origins of the concept; its role in our nation's colonial, Revolutionary, Constitutional, and subsequent history; the modern history of philanthropy in America; contemporary changes and developments, and their strategic future directions? Regardless of whether or not the particular positions argued here are accepted, the issues they address are fundamental for philanthropic studies, and students considering their futures with respect to philanthropy should have the benefit of strong instruction in these subjects.

J. Teachers

To education, as distinct from scholarship—for teachers in schools, colleges and universities professing liberal education—the New Paradigm brings new life, a true rebirth or renaissance. In the Classical view, philanthropy is a synonym for humanity. As such, it is the essence and end or goal of liberal education, and should be explicitly and systematically built-into curricula as a necessity, not a luxury or decoration. As for alumni/-ae, a philanthropic lifestyle—continuing their own self-development through value-intensive "private initiatives for public good, focusing on quality of life"—is therefore a sound criterion for testing whether a school, college or university has been successful.

These institutions should therefore be promoters of philanthropy both to their students and to their alumni/-ae. What is taught in the classroom finds beneficial usefulness through philanthropy, so teachers should take every opportunity to make that practical, beneficial, connection—to train their students to think of practical, beneficial applications of what they are learning, as a natural and necessary extension of the classroom experience in their own lives. Educational institutions' work is not completed at commencement; continuing education is also their unending task, which in the New Paradigm finds its natural expression in philanthropy, fully conceived. Therefore, alumni weekends or regional alumni-association meetings can be structured around the consideration of Classical philanthropy and the New Paradigm in philanthropy, in which the subject is not the institution's own fundraising (which would be sparsely attended in most instances), but the philanthropy of the attendees and their families—their continuing informal education through their philanthropy. These kinds of occasions would be ideal for the institutions' Alumni/-ae and Development Office staffs to assume the educational, teaching, role of faculty for philanthropy. Under those circumstances, alumni giving will certainly increase.

K. Students

Students interested in quality-of-life issues, perhaps in relation to their careers, should consider philanthropy either as a career or as an integral and essential part of their maturing lifestyles, both for themselves and in their future families.

In deciding what colleges and universities might best prepare them for these futures, and in view of the fact that a paradigm-shift is already going on in philanthropy, it is important that curricula focus on the future, and not on the immediate past, of philanthropy—on the New Paradigm and not on the Old Paradigm, on more and not less, useful knowledge.

Students should check out the curricula of colleges and universities they are considering, for whether their course offerings demonstrate awareness of the dramatic changes that are occurring, and whether they will help their students survey and prepare for their own personal or professional futures in the new world of philanthropy. This historic transformation from the 20th to the 21st century is so well and obviously under way, that there is no excuse for any curriculum's failure to express and address it. Students should be sympathetic with the difficulties and sluggishness of curricular reform, but be insistent that curricula keep up with the times, and that in this period of dramatic change in every field (not just philanthropy), colleges and universities must exhibit their awareness of the transformations that are going on in the "real" world, by keeping up with them in their academic world.

Students interested in their own self-development, and in their own values as expressive of themselves—who they are, and how the exercise of their values is the best way to define, strengthen and refine themselves—should consider that their own philanthropy is at issue as the prime criterion and instrument of self-definition, -development, and -realization. Seeing the philanthropic ramifications of knowledge is the key to one's own best education. Therefore seek out institutions, and teachers, who will work with you on that. Already, you are in the New Paradigm.

L. Journalists

Journalists generally, through no fault of their own under the Old Paradigm because it did not teach broadly, are like the public at large generally ignorant of philanthropy both conceptually and in practice. Since very little of philanthropy is primarily about money, power, or significant controversy, the media have not known where or how to cover it. Usually glittering social events are superficially reported, excessively photographed, and relegated to "society" (or the modern equivalent) pages; economic aspects appropriately find scant coverage in Business sections. There is no natural place for coverage of philanthropy, because journalists simply do not know what it is about, and "rich helping poor" is not newsworthy except in the case of celebrities, where it is interesting for celebrity, not philanthropic, reasons. This is a problem in the epistemology (the organization and validation of knowledge) of journalism—how current events and developments, should be organized for public consumption and understanding, and in particular for civic participation.

The New Paradigm can change all this, because with it the primary subject of philanthropy is quality of life. Surveys always show that everyone's highest priority is "quality of life." No one knows or cares about philanthropy, but everyone knows and cares about quality of life. People have not made the connection between the two, because we in philanthropy have not taught them to do that. No one knows or considers that while quality of life is affected by government and business, it is the focus of philanthropy, and in everyday terms it depends heavily on charitable corporations in the philanthropic sector. Religion, education, health care, the environment, cultural and human services, are all led and informed by philanthropic institutions, that are reliant on charitable giving and "private initiatives for public good."

Therefore what every newspaper, every newscast, every public broadcasting entity needs, is a "Quality of Life" section or division, to which journalists already working in other sections are assigned, with special knowledge in each of those significant fields. The distinct perspective of these sections would focus on how various private and public individuals and institutions are affecting quality of life, how they are responding to public issues concerning quality of life. In this new framework, philanthropy in all its aspects is a central and fundamental subject that can come into its own in the public mind. Again, the reason this has not been done is only that under the Old Paradigm, it was not taught. Under the New Paradigm, Internet-based tools will be available that will enormously illuminate the quality-of-life sector completely and in detail, and facilitate coverage for journalistic purposes.

For newspapers, this simple reform would boost circulation and advertising, by raising the quality and value of journalism itself, and by providing "hooks" for people and corporations in the real world—a leadership function. The epistemology of journalism is not helping circulation by focusing on the negative and on issues and events well beyond what readers can influence. By focusing on quality of life, with philanthropy prominently and necessarily involved, constructive initiatives in the life of a community acquire interest as responses to actual broad public issues and problems. The community can gain a sense of purpose, strategy, and overview by seeing how all aspects of quality of life relate to each other, and what is being done about them both within and beyond the community. Journalism would merit careful reading rather than casual surfing the fragments of reportage. The role of philanthropy or private initiatives as our early-warning system for spotting public problems and dealing with them, would be illuminated. Charitable giving and volunteering would increase, not because the stories are about charities, but because the issues and the actors would be identified. Corporations doing good work would find a public relations slot that does not now exist, that they have to make for themselves in their advertising. Everyone, already interested in quality of life, would read that section or tune-in on that part of the broadcast. Stories would pop out in ways that current (dis-)organization of news discourages.

M. Religious Leaders

Charitable giving to religious institutions is and has traditionally under the Old Paradigm been the largest (in dollars) field of giving nationwide (ca. 44-46%). This is understandable in the context of the Old Paradigm's view of charitable giving as a moral obligation.

On the other hand, that was the largest percentage in a small-percentage field—of giving as less than 2% of Gross Domestic Product and personal income.

The challenge of the New Paradigm for religious giving is whether increasing the size of the pie will also increase religion's portion of the pie, or at least the dollars involved even in a smaller percentage of the whole.

The answer lies in how religious leaders respond to the paradigm-shift. Jewish and Evangelical Protestant churches have been most successful under the

Old Paradigm in fostering religious giving. Mainline Protestant and Roman Catholic churches have been least successful. (It is arguable that Evangelical Protestant "mega-churches"—e.g., organizations like "Generous Giving"— are already in the New Paradigm, which accounts for their phenomenal success in fundraising.)

The key to the quality of the response is whether religious leaders understand that the New Paradigm solidly connects philanthropy with theology, whereas the Old Paradigm, though moralistic, was less central to religion as such. The Classical view of philanthropy historically found expression in early Christianity, and thus with the Judaeo-Christian theological tradition.

In that tradition, God was understood as philanthropic—as loving humanity. The entire Christian drama was about loving humanity. The word *philanthropia* and its cognates and related concepts were essential to the developing Christian doctrines, using the Greek word more commonly in the Greek Orthodox than its Latin equivalent *humanitas* in Roman theology and liturgy, but unmistakable in both. In the Hebrew tradition, both *tzedakah* and *tikkun olam* are essentially theological and philanthropic, and the classical authorities were Philo of Alexandria and Josephus. The theological ground is the most powerful and persuasive basis for religious philanthropy in the Western traditions. Within them, the practice of philanthropy is the good life, in harmony and unity with the ground of being itself. The Old Paradigm did not use this; its moralisms were not grounded because the ground did not matter to the technical and procedural focus. The New Paradigm, with its primary focus on substance and content as defining and authorizing subordinate procedures, can and should use its content.

This would constitute technically a "rebirth" for religious philanthropy, in the sense of revitalization by return to original roots. In these traditions, the incentives of religion would be added to those of patriotism and philanthropy.

N. Civic Leaders

The New Paradigm's focus on the Classical and historic value of philanthropy for personal and community quality of life provides a fresh rationale and clarity that the Old Paradigm lacked, as to **why** philanthropy is good citizenship, squarely within the Classical American tradition of our Founders. Those who practice "private initiatives for public good, focusing on quality of life" are Classically philanthropic, democratic, and American, promoting our civic values in their private assumption of public or civic responsibilities. Civic leadership and citizenship under the New Paradigm are not the exception but the purported norm, working to emulate and replicate the philanthropic culture that created our unique, because purportedly philanthropic, nation.

In the Old Paradigm, good citizenship was "giving back," a moral obligation. Civic leadership was more about self-sacrifice than self-fulfillment, more about corporate sacrifice than about corporate fulfillment. This negative approach guaranteed that it would be exceptional. In the New Paradigm, good citizenship is the norm—an expression of what it is to be human and American, free and democratic. Philanthropy is how a free society achieves quality of life, for which we all, individually and corporately, stand. Period.

Our nation's history has already produced a working model of a philanthropic culture, and many examples of individual philanthropic life-styles. That was how this nation was born. Our Founders defined by their inspiring examples what it is to be American and philanthropic. We can aspire to membership in that select company, by studying and following their examples. The New Paradigm creates a philanthropic culture that is positively conducive to civic leadership, and in which civic leaders teach citizenship.

O. Political Leaders

The proper relationship between philanthropy and government is partnership, in their mutual efforts to enhance quality of life in this democracy. Government needs philanthropy as society's sensory system, the first-alert to emerging public issues and problems. Philanthropy is also a society's first line of defense against problems, not only sensing them first, but responding with constructive solutions. With new problems, new solutions are often required; philanthropy is far more creative than government, and easily experiments with various problem-solving responses, to identify those that are most cost-effective. For these two reasons—greater sensitivity, and greater creativity in response—the philanthropic sector needs to operate freely and without stifling government regulation.

If an emerging social, cultural, or environmental problem continues to grow and spread despite philanthropy's best efforts, so that government intervention is necessary, philanthropy sounds the alarm, raises political support for a solution, and offers the benefit of its practical experience with the issue. Thus philanthropy helps to improve government and public policy, not just as a partner, but often enough as a leading partner. Philanthropy has continually led and set the agendas for public policies affecting quality of life. This pattern has been common throughout our colonial and national history, with every reform movement. It worked within the Old Paradigm; what can the New Paradigm contribute?

Because the New Paradigm is more articulate and positive about its substantive values, and the Classical view of philanthropy emphatically promotes democracy, freedom, and a robust philanthropic culture in society at large—which the Old Paradigm neither intended nor, perforce, accomplished—the New Paradigm awakens, ignites and promotes American idealism. This has already been demonstrated in our Revolutionary and Constitutional periods, and throughout the history of American reform movements. Therefore political leaders and government officials should welcome and support the paradigm-shift, the Classical view of philanthropy, and the New Paradigm.

Under the Old Paradigm, predictably, philanthropy was not discovered or developed as a political issue. Politicians, also predictably, are therefore woefully ignorant of philanthropy and how it works. This does not help, and actually impedes, philanthropy.

Yet we know that when philanthropy is an issue at the polls (e.g., when state-level tax incentives for charitable giving are at issue), it always wins, and by wide margins. The reasons are that philanthropy has no enemies, that every voter is a beneficiary of philanthropy, and that philanthropy is well organized for raising public awareness on issues. Politicians therefore will find it advantageous to support philanthropy not just in their charitable giving, which is increasingly scrutinized for its evidence (or not) of good character, but in their election campaigns—again, as evidence of good character. Politicians should be completely knowledgeable about philanthropic institutions and activities in their districts, well-acquainted with philanthropic leaders in their constituencies, and articulate about philanthropy's enhancement of democracy and freedom, as well as about its crucial contributions to quality of life. They should lend their authority and leadership skills to promoting philanthropy in general, and charitable giving and volunteering in particular. In the process, they will become much better informed about how philanthropy works and enhances civic health, which is after all their responsibility and obligation as leaders of the government sector, so that when issues involving philanthropy arise, their work as governors will improve.

P. Conclusion

Together, these factors suggest that a New Paradigm as outlined in previous chapters, based on the Classical view of philanthropy, especially as it was realized here in America at our nation's birth, will constitute a rebirth of American philanthropy, and of America as the world's first and foremost philanthropic nation.

To many, this may seem to be simply grandiose rhetoric, empty and vain. Whether that is merely attitudinal (in which case we may ignore it), or a substantive, well-grounded refutation of the argument of this book, we shall be very interested to see. Constructive criticism is always welcome. In the New Paradigm we are all on the same team. Let us therefore identify our common ground—what we agree on—and in that context spell out our differences, for constructive resolution and forward progress. This book is intended to promote discussion, not to conclude it.

Appendix One Case Study: The *Catalogue for Philanthropy* **System in Massachusetts:**

For the past twelve years (since 1997) an experimental project has been unfolding in Massachusetts whose history confirms and exemplifies the paradigm-shift analysis, and indicates the clear direction it is taking in Massachusetts and potentially elsewhere.

The *Catalogue* began in response to early-1990s IRS data showing that charitable giving in New England lagged behind the rest of the country, especially in comparison with income. The question was asked: Why should the wealthiest region of the country be giving the least to philanthropy? The Ellis L. Phillips Foundation of Boston, a modest family foundation (est. 1929), with a 40-year tradition of initiating projects for broader development by others, thought this was a problem they might usefully address. They formed a diverse consortium of 11 leading Massachusetts foundations, corporations and individual donors, to support a three-year, experimental donor-education Project, promoting philanthropy as a whole to Massachusetts as a whole—by itself, an innovative idea.

The centerpiece of the Project was a holiday giving-season *Catalogue for Philanthropy*, to be mailed to the top two IRS income groups (250,000 homes) statewide who then provided 51% of Massachusetts' itemized charitable contributions. The *Catalogue* was to be a showcase for excellence in philanthropy, featuring introductory articles about philanthropy, supported by brief descriptions of 100 excellent but little-known (budgets below $2 million) charities in all fields, all across the state.

The Project's initial mission was simple: "donor education, to increase and improve charitable giving." We reviewed every aspect of the interface between conventional philanthropy and the public, to see how it might be rendered more donor-friendly and conducive to giving. Almost everywhere we looked, we found inconsiderateness of or inhospitality to donors, discouraging or actually impeding donor participation.

We also noticed that powerful forces of change from outside philanthropy, were affecting it in ways that would be permanent. By 2000 we concluded that what was happening might be a paradigm-shift, and we published two articles in *Foundation News* raising that question, and asking whether traditional foundations might be marginalized if they did not adapt more quickly and adequately—by itself a significant paradigmatic change. This new historical perspective enlarged the scope of our intentions, encouraging us to pursue further innovations.

As the Project continued to innovate in response to various problematic elements in conventional philanthropy, it gradually acquired a direction and momentum of its own, creating a comprehensive Internet-based system for philanthropy in Massachusetts, that might be disseminated nationwide. In January, 2007 the *Catalogue*'s mission was amended to reflect this broader scope: "To strengthen the culture of philanthropy—its vocabulary, conceptualization, rhetoric, infrastructure, and modes of operation—through donor education and the development of innovative, donor-friendly tools designed to promote philanthropy in perpetuity." Very briefly, the various features of the new system include:

a. The *Catalogue*

The 82-page printed *Catalogue for Philanthropy* is still the cornerstone of the Project, with the same basic structure of general articles on philanthropy supported by the specific evidence of excellent charities. By 2008, 12 editions of the *Catalogue* have presented over 900 charities in all fields, statewide—the most detailed and thorough portrait of a single philanthropic market, and argument for philanthropy, ever published. Especially notable is its focus on small-to-mid-sized charities, which had previously been invisible to the public. To the extent that the Massachusetts philanthropic sector is representative, the case for philanthropy in general, and in particular our dependence on it for quality of life, is now irrefutable—no longer merely impressionistic, anecdotal, nor subject to misunderstanding or misinterpretation. Somebody, somewhere, sometime, had to make that case; it has now basically been done—and is being still further developed. A spin-off *Catalogue* in the Greater Washington D.C. region, now in its sixth year, has presented charities in a similar fashion, as have Catalogues in Whatcome County, Washington, and St. Louis, Missouri.

Initial interviews with prospective readers had elicited **unanimous** declarations that their first response to receiving such a publication would be to "wonder whether it is legitimate." "But this is philanthropy," we protested. "Exactly," came the response—"What do we know about philanthropy? Junk mail, junk telephone calls usually when we're sitting down to dinner, annual articles in the *Boston Globe* warning us to "Give, **but** Give Wisely" [the annual so-called "public relations" slogan of the Better Business Bureau and the National Society of Fund Raising Executives!], public prosecutions of crooks, and the United Way scandal." [i.e., in New York, 1990—six years earlier, but it stuck in people's minds]. This was our introduction to the challenges confronting "donor education" after a half-century's experience under the "Old Paradigm," when philanthropy was thought to be flourishing as never before. It made a strong impression.

Our experts advised that this penumbra of disrespect for philanthropy must dampen charitable giving, and had to be overcome. To do that we decided that the *Catalogue* should be a beautiful, "high-end," publication—so conspicuously high-minded, knowledgeable, well-written, eloquent, and persuasive in argument that it would render as well as state that, contrary to popular opinion, philanthropy is actually "intelligent, creative, productive, interesting, exciting, personally fulfilling, and richly varied... appealing to any interest or personal style." The 100 highly diverse charities first presented were selected from nearly 500 applicants, as "examples of excellence" in philanthropy. The first edition was distributed in prime time for holiday giving to 300,000 homes statewide, including 65,000 copies folded into a Saturday *Boston Globe*. It was unanimously praised for its high quality, subsequently winning two national Wilmer Shields Awards from the Council on Foundations, for excellence in public communications about philanthropy. (Two spin-off *Catalogues*, in Washington State and Washington D.C., also independently won the same Awards in other years. There is really nothing else of this quality out there—which is significant.)

b. The Generosity Index™
Also included in the original (1997) edition was the first broad publicity of IRS data on charitable giving and income in Massachusetts and New England. Since 1991 the *Statistics of Income Bulletin* had been publishing state-by-state summaries of the nation's income tax returns—an example of the increasing data enabled by computerization. The *Chronicle of Philanthropy* soon published the numbers, by states in alphabetic order. By the mid-'90s it began to be noticed that New England numbers were low—*e.g.*, for 1995 (the latest data available for us in 1997), the six New England states ranked 36, 44, 47, 48, 49, and 50. At first we assumed that this meant New England was relatively poor, but we found that our incomes were the highest in the country—in 1995, 1st, 3rd, 5th, 16th, 30th, and 32nd. We compared the two sets of ranks, and expressed their differences arithmetically; half had **positive** combined ranks (i.e. the giving rank was higher than the income rank), and half had **negative** combined ranks (the reverse). If the disparities between

the two ranks were themselves ranked, "in a kind of crude but telling 'Generosity Index'" (GI), where was New England? In the cellar—39th, 41st, 45th, 46th, 49th and 50th.

This was not, and we said it was not, in any sense scientific; it was merely a pedagogical exercise, illuminating and broadly publicizing IRS data to raise public conscientiousness and stimulate media discussions of charitable giving in relation to income in this country. We resurrected the conventional formulation known to fundraisers as the "widow's mite phenomenon" [*Mark* 12:41-44]—that generosity in philanthropy is not how much one gives, but how much one gives in relation to how much one has. For the public and the press, this was sensational new information.

IRS data was and is the only freely and frequently available nationwide data on income and giving. It has many technical difficulties—reporting 80% of the dollars, but only 25% (in 1995—today 30%) of taxpayers—those who itemize charitable contributions. It omits consideration of other giving and volunteering, as well as differences in costs of living or state tax burdens nationwide. As an indicator (by no means a "measure") of generosity, therefore, we called it "crude." On the other hand, we called it "telling"— because the numbers themselves are true, complete, and massive. So long as their limitations were stated, they were valid, and they offered a new, more detailed, portrait of charitable giving nationwide, showing that it is qualified by regional cultures (contiguous states tended to have similar ranks).

The Generosity Index™ attracted wide and loud attention from media columnists, who predictably responded favorably or unfavorably according to their states' ranks. In New England and Massachusetts, the majority objected to and denied it the first year, and with no further input accepted it as common knowledge the second year—the weight of the data must simply have sunk-in. The White House Council of Economic Advisors, having learned of it from an article in the *New York Times*, spent a week examining the GI for validity and included it as one of three domestic items in the *Weekly Economic Briefing of the President*, of January 9, 1998, circulated to the top 100 officials in the federal government. They kindly wrote to us, "the *Catalogue* is definitely a project that has wide-ranging ramifications."

The nationwide media loved the GI to death. Disseminated through the Associated Press system, it quickly became the nation's leading stimulus for annual discussions of charitable giving. Unfortunately, the media hardened it into an absurd "measurement" of the generosity of the entire **populations** of the various states, and from there it was politicized, adding insult to injury by alleging it to show that "Red" conservative states are more generous than "Blue" liberal states. Our protestations, denials and qualifications had no effect, so we abandoned it in 2005. Live, and learn.

On the positive side, however, the media's discussions of charitable giving increased in both number and quality. The notion that philanthropic generosity is the relation of giving to income or wealth was readily accepted; and the public discussions of charitable giving actually increased giving.

What happened to charitable giving in Massachusetts? From 1991-6, Massachusetts had ranked dead last—50th—in the GI. In 1997, the year the story broke, Massachusetts donors reacted as sensible adults to the new feedback, and increased their giving. Our GI suddenly jumped to 47th, and by 2000, in only four years, we had nearly doubled our total charitable giving, roughly from $2 billion to $4 billion. The increase was accomplished entirely by the top income group, which was also the *Catalogue*'s audience. The *Catalogue* makes no claims for this success, but it is clear that something unique was happening in Massachusetts. From 1997-2000, nationwide, income increased 38.5% while giving increased by 62.2%; **Massachusetts'** income increased at about the same rate (39%), but our **giving increased by more than half again as much—96.5%—**and much more than the next highest state (ca. 80%). In 2001-3 the economic recession and 9/11 took the wind out of everyone's sails, but Massachusetts never fell back to its previous low giving levels. By 2004 we had regained almost the entire setback, and in 2005 we exceeded our previous record (2000) by 10%. Massachusetts seems now to be permanently out of its Old-Paradigm doldrums.

Strategically, the *Catalogue* Project has concluded that increasing charitable giving is not difficult. Of course it was low to begin with, and no one was working on it. In the Old Paradigm, increasing charitable giving was—to our great surprise— no one's job, nor any institution's mission. The sector was fragmented, and every charity promoted giving only to itself; no one was speaking for philanthropy as a whole. When, with the GI, local media interviewed professionals on charitable giving, they found no experts on the subject. Instead, they could only find individual charities talking about their own experiences, or at best community foundations who said nice things about their communities, with no particular data to back them up. Heads of Regional Associations of Grantmakers, or of local chapters of the National Society of Fundraisers, were not routinely consulted for well-informed, data-rich, comments. This, too, made a strong impression on us.

c. State Giving Days:

This modest and as yet unfulfilled element in the *Catalogue*'s program, nonetheless illustrates the development of our thinking about the Old and New Paradigms, about the greater significance of philanthropy in American history, and in particular about fundraising as donor education—teaching and promoting philanthropy.

The Association of Fundraising Professionals (AFP—then called the National Society of Fund Raising Executives, or NSFRE) annually declares a "National Philanthropy Day" on November 15, leaving to local and State chapters the option of designating more convenient days around that time. The occasion focuses only on fundraising—the beginning of the year-end "prime time" annual appeals, with the secondary theme of timeliness for gaining tax-incentives.

Almost immediately the *Catalogue* discovered that our more historically and etymologically accurate definition of philanthropy opened up a new understanding of its profound role in American history. In 1998 we included a brief article on the history and meaning of the 17th-century English concept of "Commonwealth" (originally applied to the Massachusetts, Pennsylvania and Virginia colonies), showing that it contained the notion of philanthropy. In 1999 we outlined the argument of Chapter II above, and "to help teach all this," proposed that National Philanthropy Day be connected with Thanksgiving or the day after, when families are together and gratefully mindful of their bounty in America. Just as in the 20th century Americans had learned to telephone their mothers on Mothers' Day, so in the 21st century families who were already together on Thanksgiving weekend might learn to log onto the Internet, to do their annual charitable giving—to "Give Thanks by Giving." We approached the Massachusetts chapter and the national Board of AFP with the idea, but they were not interested; so we proceeded on our own to test it.

The first State Giving Day was declared as the day after Thanksgiving in 2002 by Acting Governor Jane Swift of Massachusetts. Her declaration read:

> **WHEREAS:** The nation's First Thanksgiving took place here in Massachusetts, and

WHEREAS: the first "recommendation" that there be a Thursday "set apart...for solemn thanksgiving and praise, that with one heart and one voice the good people may express the grateful feelings of their hearts and consecrate themselves to the service of their divine benefactor...." [n.b.] was proposed on November 1, 1777 by Samuel Adams, a Son of Massachusetts, and later adopted by the 13 states as the first official Thanksgiving Proclamation, and

WHEREAS: Philanthropy—"private initiatives for the public good, focusing on quality of life"— is both essential to civic health in self-governing societies, and generally recognized as an appropriate expression of gratitude on the part of donors for the benefits they enjoy in life, and

WHEREAS: Massachusetts citizens have been steadily increasing our charitable giving so that we now lead the nation in the rate of increase in giving, and finally

WHEREAS: our citizens should be commended for their philanthropy, and encouraged to sustain its growth in partnership with government [n.b.] as together we seek to enhance the quality of life for all our citizens,

NOW, THEREFORE, I, JANE SWIFT, Governor of the Commonwealth of Massachusetts, do hereby proclaim the Friday after Thanksgiving, November 29, 2002, to be

GIVING MASSACHUSETTS DAY

and urge all the citizens of the Commonwealth to take cognizance of this event and participate fittingly in its observance.

The practical and procedural purpose of State Giving Days is to fortify annual fundraising appeals of all charities—by giving the media a handle to remind everyone to respond to the appeal letters; and by identifying an interesting occasion—families together, in the spirit of Thanksgiving—in which to do so. Substantively, the Proclamation raises consciousness about philanthropy's essential relation to our national history and the quality of life we celebrate on Thanksgiving; it creates an occasion in which government officials actually promote philanthropy and in which government and philanthropy work together as partners—a win-win political situation.

The State Giving Days idea, like the GI but on a smaller scale, took on a life of its own, with modest assists from us. Rhode Island adopted it within a week. New Hampshire joined in 2003. By 2006 eleven states' governors across the country had signed proclamations, and the media were discussing it favorably in 27 other states. To do it well, however, requires careful preparation with charities, community foundations, and the media, and we have had neither the staff nor the time to develop it. The tool is available; governors are happy to respond to requests to do this from local charities, and it does resonate.

d. The *Catalogue* Website and "*Catalogue*-in-a-Box"

The *Catalogue* Project took several years to move to the Internet. In 1997 few small-to-mid-sized charities had their own websites, but we assumed that the *Catalogue* would move to the Web at some point. We first publicized our website in 1998, but it was not fully functional for giving until 2001. In 2002 we began to use it administratively with our database; in 2003 we began haltingly to feature and track electronic giving. In 2004 we used it to streamline our application and selection process for charities' listings.

It was also obvious to everyone from the outset that the *Catalogue* Project would have broader applications beyond Massachusetts and our own website, so the phrase "*Catalogue*-in-a-Box" appeared in our lexicon, signifying webware tools we would devise for ourselves, which would also be modular and licensable by other communities and markets, to facilitate dissemination of the *Catalogue* model. With Internet technology, any community or state could create their own web-based *Catalogue* system at very low cost, fortified by some sort of hardcopy outreach piece to attract visitors to the websites.

The first demonstration of the value in our proposal solicitation-and-review process occurred in Massachusetts, when newly-elected Governor Deval Patrick decided to allocate his Inaugural surplus funds to philanthropic grants. The Inaugural Committee chose to emulate our focus on small-to-mid-sized charities in all fields, all across the state, so we offered to loan them our webware for their process. We casually told them it would accommodate any number of reviewers, and they surprised us by inviting 1,000 prominent Patrick supporters all across the state to serve on the review panel! Of those, 500 accepted! We and, at our suggestion the community foundations of Massachusetts, assisted in encouraging applicants, and 1750 charities applied! This produced, in flex-time for reviewers' convenience, 10,000 individual proposal reviews, using our system of scoring and commenting on each one. Our webware guided their reviewers for maximum coverage, and our built-in taxonomy organized the proposals and their reviews by fields. The webware ranked applicants' scores in each field so that a smaller final selection committee could simply choose the top scorers in each field, working down each list until they had the number they needed. They awarded 215 grants for excellence in philanthropy, equitably distributed across all fields, all across the state. The entire process took only a few weeks and was accomplished flawlessly, by people generally inexperienced in philanthropy.

Once again, this Project exemplified the New Paradigm model of government promoting philanthropy as an equal partner. The reviewers, who were political supporters of the Governor's, gained an "inside" understanding of how philanthropy works, and from the applications they read, of the excellence that is common in philanthropy. Since this demonstration, corporations and community foundations have approached us to use this broadly participatory, highly efficient, web-based system.

e. The *Directories*

When the *Catalogue* Project began in 1997, knowledge about philanthropy and the philanthropic sector in Massachusetts (and everywhere) was primitive—confined to whatever was more or less accidentally known by individuals or individual institutions, gathered in their own ways for their own purposes. There was no organized, growing, developing, common body of knowledge shared by the Massachusetts philanthropic community in its mutual enterprise, nor by an academic community dedicated to its study.

One might reasonably expect, after a half-century of dramatic growth, professionalization, and maturation as a field of endeavor, that the philanthropic sector would be understood in at least basic terms—that we would all know how many charities there are, into what fields they are divided, and perhaps what basic types of organizations exist. In fact, none of these has been a particular concern, or is known, much less agreed-upon. This lack of basic knowledge illustrates and proves the Old Paradigm's lack of interest in philanthropy as a whole. It is entirely consistent with the fragmentation of the sector into separate parts, with the rare usage of the word itself. Such primitive conditions prevent the development of a strong national culture of philanthropy.

The *Catalogue* needed a complete list of Massachusetts charities, to invite applications for listing from everyone (for equitability's sake). GuideStar, the national on-line database founded in 1994 in response to the lack of organized knowledge of charities, was not yet sufficiently developed. We therefore collaborated with the state's community foundations, whose combined lists were the closest approximation to completeness. We were told by various sources that there might be about 7-11,000 charities eligible—incorporated in Massachusetts, in all fields, with budgets below $2 million (our limit 1997-2005). Over the next few years GuideStar became stronger and our friendly colleague Buzz Schmidt, its founder and then CEO, generously shared his data with us.

Then the IRS made its Form 990s available to the public on-line, and we moved gradually toward composing our own list of eligible charities from those two resources. In 2005 we downloaded the IRS data on "non-profits" ourselves. By pruning the most obviously inappropriate groups—clubs, lobbyists, professional associations, etc.—we came up with a tentative list of about 7,000 "non-profits" thought to be eligible. Given the cost of a mailing that size, however, we glanced down it and noticed immediately that it could be pruned still further, so we continued, one-by-one, designating their fields with our taxonomy as we went.

Some were classifiable as to eligibility and field by their name alone; many were not, but for those the fast-growing Google could provide their websites, which we could check with a click. It is important that before computers, the Internet, and fully mature Google, it was impossible to do what we were doing—which is the main reason why it had never been done.

1. Typology
But another reason this kind of detailed scrutiny had never been done anywhere was a remarkable and telling lack of institutional inclination. Before the *Catalogue* there was no institution, nor anyone's job, that needed or wanted both comprehensive and detailed knowledge of the sector. It took us eight years to get around to it, and when we did the critical decision was accidental, relating to postage costs. But the combination of improving technology and rising postage costs produced the necessity that mothered this invention.

Our first discovery was that **philanthropic** "non-profits" are of four significantly different operating types: 1) those of **internal** interest—*e.g.*, clubs, religious congregations, etc.—that exist for and serve their members, who know about and support them; 2) those of **local** interest—serving and being supported by their local communities, who generally know about them; 3) those of **general** interest—addressing broad public issues and fundraising from the general public, who generally do not know them (the iceberg phenomenon); and 4) a few large and well-known charities that have all the above traits plus others relating to their size and scope.

For the *Catalogue*'s donor-education purposes, obviously the third group is of greatest relevance—interest and value—to donors, grantmakers, and philanthropic advisors statewide; they are also what most people think of as "philanthropy."

But beyond the *Catalogue*'s concerns, this typology—which is immaterial to, and thus never developed by, the IRS—is significant for many analytical, strategic, and practical purposes in philanthropy. Each type of institution has characteristic needs, concerns, values, challenges, opportunities, internal and external resources, styles, modes of operation, life-cycles, personal and institutional networks, institutional development trajectories, etc. A charity's characteristic type determines a great deal about its existence, history, clients and benefits, staff and their careers, as well as its contributions to quality of life in society—and each type relates to a distinct "society" (the membership, the community, the general public, or all three). But again, because the typology is of no interest or relevance to the IRS for its purposes, IRS data ignores it—another reason why IRS data must be refined for practical utility in philanthropy.

2. Numbers

The typology revealed that the number of charities eligible for the *Catalogue*—i.e., those of general philanthropic interest with budgets below $3 million (raised in 2005), comprising 90% of all Massachusetts general-interest charities—is far smaller than anyone had suspected: about 2,600, statewide, out of the original 7,000.

This is not to say that charities of local interest (to their neighbors) or internal interest (to their members) are not philanthropic—they are certainly so, as a matter of fact and public policy. Generally, they have much smaller budgets, staffs and impacts; we plan to develop a *Directory* for those of equal interest as well.

Breadth of philanthropic interest is not determined by field or kind of activity, but by the scope of the issues addressed. A day-care center in a wealthy suburb is not of broad philanthropic interest, whereas one in an inner city or disadvantaged rural area might well be of interest to donors statewide—because they are concerned with the broad issue of social change. A land trust conserving open space in a suburb is not of general philanthropic interest unless, for example, it has a rare or endangered plant species among its flora, in which case it concerns biodiversity conservation, invoking state and possibly federal regulation. Because breadth of philanthropic interest is a function of multiple factors, including donors' interests, classification by type can be a judgment-call. The *Catalogue* is therefore developing its typological classifications in collaboration with the charities themselves, to arrive at a fair consensus. In the New Paradigm we are all on the same team; this far more detailed portrait of the Massachusetts philanthropic sector is being developed for everyone's free access and use—donors, grantmakers, philanthropic advisors, strategists, media journalists, scholars, students, *et al.*

The whole issue of numbers and size of the sector and its parts makes all the difference in the world to our knowledge, understanding, and strategizing in philanthropy. The fact is that the Massachusetts experience shows that our entire sector needs a detailed census in every market; we now have the tools with which to do that; and until we do it we are stumbling around in the dark.

3. Taxonomy of Fields

The designation of fields is not easy intellectually, and was technologically impossible to describe graphically under the Old Paradigm, which represented things on paper, in only two dimensions. There are innumerable names and lists of fields of philanthropy, *e.g.*, in directories of grantmakers and their funding interests. But because the categories in these lists are not systematically or logically related to each other, the lists are not, strictly speaking, "taxonomies." Partly owing to this informality they vary widely and randomly from place to place and time to time, which prevents their comparative use or synthesis in data collection and analysis, and especially between and among philanthropic markets nationwide. If fields are not systematically or logically connected to each other, gaps or incompatibilities between them prevent easy navigation or exploration by discoverers—which means donors, grantmakers, journalists, scholars, students, etc.

From our first edition in 1997, therefore, the *Catalogue* felt it necessary to develop a donor-friendly taxonomy of fields, to help donors find charities they would like to support, as well as for our own data collection and analyses. For only 100 charities, even adding roughly 100 more each year, defining fields systematically was relatively easy. We based ours on three fundamental, irreducible, therefore extremely stable, areas of both philanthropy and quality of life: "Nature": etymologically, what is born—the given, material environment in which humans live; "Culture": etymologically, what is artificially made or grown—what humans create; and "Human Services": what humans do for each other. Each of these basic fields then divides and subdivides logically, in successive stages, into increasingly specific constituent parts. (see Taxonomic Tree, Appendix Two, p.170–171.)

By 2008 the *Catalogue* family of charities, showcasing "excellence in philanthropy" had grown to over 900—approximately one-third of the entire group of charities of general interest with budgets below $3 million. Representing them taxonomically had become increasingly complex, especially in Human Services. We were bumping up against the limits of technical possibility. We had already declared our intention to publish, on our website, complete *Directories* to all the charities in Massachusetts of interest to donors: those of 1) general and 2) local interest, and to complete the system, of 3) the largest and best-known institutions. How could our taxonomy encompass all 2600 charities in the first *Directory*? Given that they would be posted on our website, we considered state-of-the-art Web 2.0 possibilities.

4. The *Directories* System
Philanthropy under the Old Paradigm, as defined by IRS data, might as well have been *terra incognita* for practical purposes in philanthropy. If we can classify the total number in terms of what **types** of organizations they are, distinct sets of strategies emerge for each type. If we can **define their fields** systematically, as connected in a coherent whole system, it is open to navigation, exploration, and teaching. If we can then count them field by field, the fields emerge—**for the first time**—as compassable entities. We can get our arms around them because we know what fields there are, and how many charities are in each one; and because these numbers are small, they are approachable and manageable. The three basic steps we took to simplify our mailing list, thus had opened up innumerable strategic possibilities for every constituency in philanthropy—donors, grantmakers, philanthropic advisors, managers of charities, journalists, scholars, students, etc. With Web 2.0 technology, we could present this new portrait of the sector in many dimensions at once. This opportunity lifted the *Directories* Project to a new strategic plateau—new, in fact, for philanthropy.

With Old Paradigm two-dimensional print technology we could have published a telephone-directory type of alphabetical list of charities, by name, with their street addresses, telephone numbers, and even website addresses. We would obtain this information from the IRS 990s, which we could download annually and translate onto a spreadsheet, substituting or adding to the IRS' our own taxonomic field designations. If our subject were the individual charities (as the telephone directory's is individual telephone numbers), this would be as adequate and as exciting as telephone directories are. Donors could find individual charities' information if they already knew the names of the charities. Further lists could be produced by sorting for each column—by field, or by geographic areas.

Suppose, however, we included additional useful data from the 990s: budget size and date of IRS authorization. Suppose we added to this information from their websites, kinds of people served—by gender, stage of life, race, and ethnicity. Suppose further that with Web 2.0 interactivity we made all these parameters interactive, and displayed them graphically, to be manipulated with cursors. Then a user could designate a field of philanthropy on the graphic schematic tree of fields; define a geographic area by outlining it on a map of Massachusetts that magnified and elaborated in greater detail as the map was zoomed; define a range of budget sizes along a line; define a range of IRS authorization dates (as indicators of institutional maturity) along another line; define the demographics of people served on another graphic element; and in a window would appear the number of charities meeting those parameters. If the user wanted to adjust any of the parameters, the number of charities would change. When the parameters were set to the user's satisfaction, a click on the number would drop down a list of the charities so designated, with their website addresses and community foundation region for further detailed reference. Each charity's parameters would be displayed for comparisons.

If the user is a donor, grantmaker, or philanthropic advisor, searching for one or more charities to consider comparatively or as a group for strategic investments, this technology renders objective, complete, and systematic, what has been a relatively subjective, incomplete, and accidental inquiry—based on what people who happen to be known, know about charities they happen to know. Here the dataset is all charities that exist within designated objective parameters. The user has complete command of the data to be considered.

Here however a new subject emerges for consideration: whole fields. Heretofore this has been impossible—because the national lists are not systematic, coherent, or rational; and because the field names and relations are not donor-friendly—in ordinary English, connecting them logically (the emphasis has been on separation, not connection). We expect that the emergence of fields as subjects of interest, development, and investment, will **encourage and increase strategic investments in philanthropy.** This is a technology-enabled, fundamental, irreversible, structural and strategic, change—a paradigmatic change.

Let us consider some examples:

If the user is a practical strategist within a particular field, this new instrument allows for the first time a means of readily analyzing whole fields structurally and strategically. Leaders and managers in fields might be convened in the presence of interested donors and grantmakers, to discuss the data on the website, to identify issues of concern, possible field-development strategies in response, and indications of potential interest by investors in the problem-solving. "Field Development Programs" become routine possibilities—a significant strategic advance.

If the user is a scholar, journalist, or student, curious to know about a **field** of philanthropy—a line of inquiry impossible under the Old Paradigm—one could designate the field on the taxonomic tree, all budget sizes on that line, the geographic area of interest on the map (the whole state?), whatever demographics are relevant, and slide the cursor along the timeline of IRS authorizations, and watch the history of the field unfold—see charities multiply and spread across the area, at each step showing all that existed at that point in time, amenable to analyses by the other parameters (e.g. numbers, budget sizes, geographical distribution, populations served), supplemented by each charity's history as described on their websites. The **history** of **every** field can now be portrayed and studied, and the history of individual charities can be seen in the historical contexts of their fields. This opening-up of the history of philanthropy, field by field, is entirely new and transforming.

Suppose the "user" is a community, wanting to know, describe, understand, and analyze its own philanthropic resources—even their history. For simplicity's and clarity's sake, let's consider an island: Martha's Vineyard, or Nantucket. That area is designated; all budget sizes, all populations, all fields. By sliding the cursor along the timeline, the history of philanthropy in the community would unfold—the total number at any date would appear in the window, the list of charities could drop-down—a snapshot of the community's philanthropic resources developing through time.

The next step would be **entirely new**—not just all charities in all fields current, but because the fields covered are depicted on the taxonomic tree, the community could see graphically what **fields** of philanthropy are **missing—not represented**! Never before have communities been able to see, systematically and completely, what philanthropic resources they **lack**. The question has not even occurred to anyone, because the next step beyond a comprehensive survey of existing charities—to what charities do not exist, cannot be asked without complete data and a systematic taxonomy. This enables communities to develop their philanthropic resources strategically—a whole new field of endeavor.

For example, they might lack a domestic violence and sexual abuse shelter; they could search surrounding communities to find the nearest one, and either include them in a community directory (downloadable from our website), or financially support an extension of their services to this community, or create a satellite operation in their own community, under the aegis of the neighboring charity. Community philanthropic development is thus created as a systematic and strategic option.

With this powerful instrument, there will no longer be any excuse for the media's well-known and highly conspicuous ignorance of philanthropy. Scholars will have an enormous new source and body of data so they can easily do the basic research that will adequately describe philanthropy and its contributions to quality of life in our society and culture. Master's essays and doctoral dissertations will pop out of this new data.

As the word spreads about how advantageous and beneficial this innovation is for Massachusetts, it is certain to be replicated or adapted nationwide. We shall actively promote its dissemination by designing the webware in modular forms, for licensing to other markets (to help pay for the substantial initial investment we are making to conceive, design, and produce it).

What this means is that philanthropy, powered by new technology of the Internet, is on the verge of becoming systematic. Many innovations will be tried and tested by experience. With this Project, Massachusetts is leading the way and inevitably setting precedents and standards for practical utility and value. We intend to encourage other colleagues and innovators to work with us "to strengthen the culture of philanthropy."

Appendix Two: A Taxonomic Tree of Philanthropy

There are innumerable lists of fields in philanthropy, usually associated with directories of grantmakers and their funding interests; but because the categories are not systematic— i.e., logically related—the lists are technically not taxonomies. This reduces their value in donor education, in data collection and analysis, and in strategic planning and management. The lists themselves are inherently ephemeral, and generally a missed opportunity, however temporarily convenient.

From the outset therefore, the *Catalogue for Philanthropy* developed its own taxonomy to help illuminate philanthropy for donors. It is based on three fundamental, irreducible, and thus extremely stable, areas of both philanthropy and quality of life: "Nature"—the given material and biological environment in which humans live; "Culture"—what humans cultivate, make, grow, or create; and "Human Services"—what humans do for each other.

To our knowledge, this taxonomic tree is the first graphic representation of all of philanthropy, as a coherent whole. Our choice of a living tree as the metaphor is not just owing to schematic tradition—of branches deriving from a main trunk—but to suggest that philanthropy is organic, alive and growing naturally, becoming ever more variegated and specialized through time.

This map of philanthropy also illustrates and connects objective aspects or dimensions of quality of life, which is also an organic whole of integrated and interdependent parts.

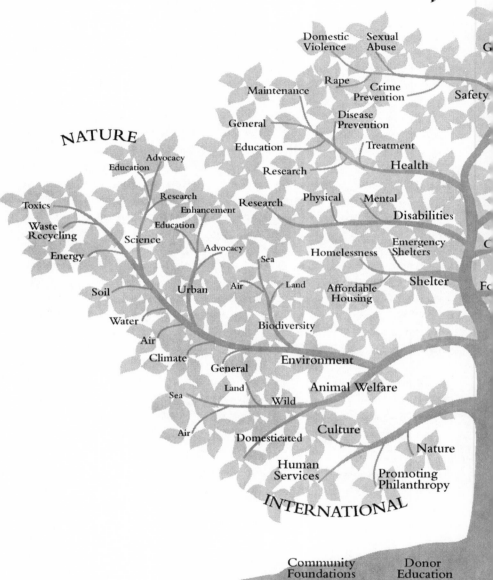

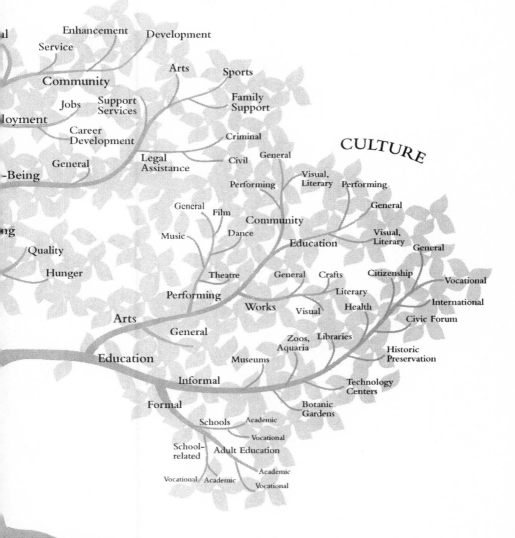

ERVICES

Enhancement Development
Service
                    Arts   Sports
Community
        Jobs   Support   Family
              Services   Support
loyment
        Career   Criminal   CULTURE
        Development
                                    General
        General   Legal   Civil
-Being   Assistance   General
                          Performing   Visual,
                                        Literary Performing
                    General Film   General
ng   Community
        Quality   Music Dance   Visual,
                                    Education Literary   General
        Hunger
                    Theatre   General Crafts Citizenship
                                                          Vocational
              Performing   Literary
        Arts   Works   Visual   Health   International
              General   Civic Forum
                                Zoos, Libraries
                                Aquaria   Historic
        Education   Museums   Preservation
                    Informal
                                        Technology
              Formal   Centers
                    Schools Academic   Botanic
                                        Gardens
              School-   Vocational
              related   Adult Education
                              Academic
              Vocational Academic
                              Vocational

ritable   Technical
iving   Assistance

ANTHROPY

Illustration by Susanah Howland, 2007

Appendix Three: Bibliographical Notes

The various ideas comprising the argument of this book have all originated in articles I have written for the *Catalogue for Philanthropy,* vols. I-XII,
1997-2008. Many have been discussed in talks or occasional articles elsewhere.
These Notes are bibliographic supplements to the various chapters, indicat-
ing works I have found particularly useful and for which I am grateful.

I. Promethean Fire: The Archetype

This chapter does not presume to contribute to scholarship in Classics; it
basically represents my own reflections on this subject over the past 25
years, which I have presented many times in various forms in and outside
the *Catalogue,* one of which was recently anthologized in Amy Kass, ed.
Giving Well, Doing Good (Indiana UP, 2008), pp. 423-5. Though the coinage
in *Prometheus Bound* has been generally known (I first learned of it decades
ago in a standard encyclopedia), and there is a modest scholarly literature on
it, I did not run across any extended discussion of it by a trained specialist,
in connection with modern philanthropy, until Marty Sulek's "Philosophia
and Philanthropia: A Cultural History of the Interrelations between Philosophy and Philanthropy from the Pre-Socratics to the Post-Moderns,"
(ARNOVA Conference, November 16-18, 2006, Chicago IL), which is a
summary of his 2003 Master's Thesis at Indiana University. Marty has been
kind enough to share this and subsequent papers of his with me, including:
"On the Meaning of Philanthropy Classical and Modern" (originally for the
Indiana University Center on Philanthropy, Workshop in Multidisciplinary
Philanthropic Studies, April 1, 2008), which is being revised for publica-
tion in the *Nonprofit and Voluntary Sector Quarterly,* and "The Promethean
Myth in Greek Poetry and Philosophy," to be presented at the ARNOVA
conference in November, 2008. There seems to be a surge of interest among
Classicists in the concept of *philanthropia*—e.g., a symposium at DePauw
University, March 16-18, 2007, on "Graeco-Roman Philanthropy and
Christian Charity"—as well as increasingly broad progress in a humanistic
understanding of the field of philanthropic studies. See Thomas Jeavons'
columns in the ARNOVA Newsletter, and articles by Nancy Goldfarb.

See also: Richard A. Bauman, *Human Rights in Ancient Rome* (Routledge,
2000); Birger Pearson: *Ancient Roots of Western Philanthropy,* (Indiana Center
on Philanthropy, 1997); Pierre Hadot, *What is Ancient Philosophy?* (tr. Michael Chase, Harvard, 2002); and Werner Jaeger, *Paideia,* 3 vols. (Oxford,
1939-1945).

II. Philanthropy's Finest Hours: the American Revolution

It is not surprising, and certainly not their fault, that American historians working in a period when professional philanthropists ignored the Classical view of philanthropy, did not grasp the significance of Classical philanthropy and philanthropic voluntary associations in the American Revolution and Constitution periods—nor that professional philanthropists did not grasp the significance for philanthropy of the philanthropic intensity of our birth as a nation. Nor is it surprising that these connections would readily occur to someone interested in all three fields, of Classical culture, American history, and American philanthropy today. They are implicit throughout the standard literature. There are many more places to look than can be cited here, but I have especially valued Garry Wills' treatment of the "pursuit of happiness" in *Inventing America: Jefferson's Declaration of Independence* (Doubleday, 1978); Hans J. Morgenthau's *The Purpose of American Politics* (Random House, 1960); Henry Steele Commager's *The Empire of Reason: How Europe Imagined and America Realized the Enlightenment* (Doubleday, 1977); Carl Becker's *The Declaration of Independence* (Smith Peter, 1979); and on the Scottish Enlightenment, Arthur Herman, *How the Scots Invented the Modern World* (Random House, 2001).

Owing to the knowledge and teaching gap noted above, the best biographies of Ben Franklin, by four leading historians, have not adequately recognized and appreciated his philanthropy, either in his own life, or in the life of his country, in his time or in ours. That said, these are wonderful books and I have found them immensely valuable; they are: the standard biography by H.W. Brands, *The First American: The Life and Times of Benjamin Franklin* (Doubleday, 2000); and three short summaries written for the tricentennial of Franklin's birth in 2006: Walter Isaacson: *Benjamin Franklin: An American Life* (Simon & Schuster, 2004); Edmund S. Morgan: *Benjamin Franklin* (Yale, 2002); and Gordon S. Wood: *The Americanization of Benjamin Franklin* (Penguin, 2004). The same condition weakens Wood's *Revolutionary Characters—What Made the Founders Different* (Penguin, 2006), which cites "high-minded rhetoric" and "civic spirit" as significant attributes in the literature of the times, but never philanthropy, nor voluntary associations, nor perforce their connection, nor the possibility that Classical philanthropy was the main "difference." On Paul Revere I have cited in this chapter David Hackett Fischer's, *Paul Revere's Ride* (Oxford, 1994). Both Franklin and Revere attested to the decisive influence of Cotton Mather's classic of 1710, *Bonifacius: An Essay...to Do Good*, which I have also cited. The classic treatment of the role of philanthropy in American history is still Robert

Bremner's *American Philanthropy* (Chicago, 1960, 1988), but it completely fails to grasp the point that the founding of this nation was the product and principal achievement of Classical philanthropy through voluntary associations. Richard C. Cornuelle's tendentious *Reclaiming the American Dream—The Role of Private Individuals and Voluntary Associations* (Random House, 1965; Rutgers, 1993) is pertinent, though I liked the title better than the book. The classic appreciation of voluntary associations in our early history, though without detailed historical analysis, is Alexis de Tocqueville's *Democracy in America* (1835, 1840, the best modern edition of which is Library of America, 2004). The classic formulation of political revolution is in R.R. Palmer's magisterial *The Age of the Democratic Revolutions* (Princeton, 2 vols., 1959, 1964). Among modern anthologies, I have especially valued Brian O'Connell's *America's Voluntary Spirit* (The Foundation Center, 1983), Amy Kass' *The Perfect Gift: The Philanthropic Imagination in Poetry and Prose* (Indiana, 2002) and her *Giving Well, Doing Good Readings for Thoughtful Philanthropists* (Indiana, 2008).

III. Philanthropy Yesterday and Today: Paradigm-Formation and -Shift, and IV. The Future of Philanthropy

To my knowledge, this chapter and the next are the first extended analysis of American philanthropy's recent history as the maturation of a paradigmatic field, now undergoing paradigm-shift. The concept and role of paradigms in the histories of fields originated in Thomas Kuhn's work in the history of early-modern science, particularly *The Copernican Revolution* (Harvard, 1959) and *The Structure of Scientific Revolutions* (Chicago, 1962). Though originally controversial, his terminology has since passed into the vernacular, with a corresponding decline in precision and rigor. Here his concept is elaborated into a systematic methodology, to assist analysis in the relatively disorderly midst of a paradigm-shift.

My knowledge and understanding of the period is based on my own professional experience living and working through it, rather than on extensive reading alone; I acknowledge that this method has the characteristic strengths and weaknesses of a primary source (the direct account of an eye-witness), as compared with a secondary source (studies based on primary sources). I have published earlier versions of this analysis in *Foundation News and Commentary* (Council on Foundations, March–April and September–October, 2000); subsequent developments have confirmed it.

My reading during this time has been casual and episodic—dipping into professional sources as they appeared—rather than concerted and scholarly.

V. Philanthropy Reborn

For similar reasons, this chapter presents my own reflections and hypotheses as distinct from those of others, so there are no particular readings I can recommend. A significant difference, perhaps, is that this chapter attempts a more comprehensive view of the future of American philanthropy, rather than particular speculation on this or that aspect of the future. Because its various aspects are interconnected, because interdependent, they exert a certain discipline on each other, increasing the probabilities that they will actually come to be. Recalling this book's view of causation in history as the "coincidence of mutually conducive conditions," what is projected for each of the various constituencies described, are collectively mutually conducive to the other projections. What happens to donors will interact with and influence what happens to fundraisers, and vice-versa. If any one of them turns out to take a dramatically different course than what is foreseen here, that will affect all or most of the others. As with all plans and projections, whose use is to guide future activity, this should be regarded as a work-in-progress, for which mid-course corrections are encouraged as unforeseen contingencies arise.

Printed in the United States
126107LV00006B/246/P